HEINEMANN HISTORY

THE MEDIEVAL REALMS

STUDY UNITS

West Leeds High School
Congress Mount
Leeds LS12 3DT

HEINEMANN
EDUCATIONAL

Nigel Kelly

Heinemann Educational Publishers
Halley Court, Jordan Hill, Oxford OX2 8EJ
a division of Reed Educational & Professional
Publishing Ltd

MELBOURNE AUCKLAND
FLORENCE PRAGUE MADRID ATHENS
SINGAPORE TOKYO SAO PAULO
CHICAGO PORTSMOUTH (NH) MEXICO
IBADAN GABORONE JOHANNESBURG
KAMPALA NAIROBI

First published 1991
96 97 98   17 16 15 14 13 12 11
British Library Cataloguing in Publication Data

Kelly, Nigel 1954–
    The medieval realms.
    1. Great Britain, history, 1066–1485
    I. Title
941.02

ISBN 0-435-31278-2

Designed by Ron Kamen, Green Door Design Ltd,
Basingstoke

Illustrated by Jeff Edwards Douglas Hall
Stuart Hughes Terry Thomas

Printed in China

Acknowledgements

The author and publisher would like to thank the following
for permission to reproduce photographs:

Bibliothèque National: 4.1B, 4.2B, 4.7E, 5.1C
Bibliothèque Royale Albert, Brussels: 5.2C
Bodleian Library: 3.8A, 4.2B, 5.1C
British Library: 3.2B, C, D and E, 3.8B, 4.1A, 4.2A and D,
4.3B, 4.4B, 4.5A and B, 4.6B, 4.7D and F, 4.8A and D, 5.3F,
5.4A and E
The Trustees of the British Museum: 1.1A
Cadw: Welsh Historic Monuments. Crown Copyright: 3.7C
Cambridge University Library: 4.8B
Cambridge University Technical Services Ltd: 2.5C
J. Allan Cash Ltd: 1.1C
The Dean and Chapter of Durham: 2.4B
Mary Evans Picture Library: 4.9D
English Heritage: 2.6A
Giraudon: 4.6A
Sonia Halliday Photographs: 3.3C
Hastings Tourism and Leisure Department: 3.4B
Michael Holford: 1.1D, 2.1A, 2.2A and B
Lauros-Giraudon: 4.7A
Mansell Collection: 2.3C
Sealand Aerial Photography: 2.5A
Source Photographic Archives: 3.6D
Trinity College, Cambridge: 4.4A, 4.5C, D and E

Woodsmansterne Ltd/Nicholas Servian: 4.3A
Source 3.5A is reproduced from a former edition of the
Ladybird title *Kings and Queens Volume I*, illustrated by Frank
Hampson with permission of the publishers, Ladybird Books
Ltd.
Cover photograph by C. M. Dixon

Details of Written Sources

In some sources the wording or sentence structure has been
simplified to ensure that the source is accessible.

R. Barber, *A Strong Land and a Sturdy*, Deutsch, 1976: 4.8F
Norman Cohn, The Pursuit of the Millennium, Paladin,
1970: 3.3A
G. G. Coulton, *Medieval Panorama II: The Horizons of
Thought*, Cambridge University Press, 1938: 4.8E
C. Culpin, *Past Into Present 1*, Collins Educational, 1988:
5.1D
R. B. Dobson, *The Peasants Revolt of 1381*, Macmillan, 1970:
5.3A, B, C, D and E, 5.4B, C and D
A. A. Erskine and A. L. Davidson, *Scotland at Peace, At War,
1263–1329*, Edward Arnold, 1978: 3.8C
G. N. Garmonsway (Trans.), *The Anglo-Saxon Chronicle*, J. M.
Dent & Sons Ltd, 1953: 2.7A
J. A. Giles (Ed.) *William of Malmesbury's Chronicle of the Kings
of England*, Henry Bohun, 1847: 2.3B
Elizabeth Hallam (Ed.), *Chronicles of the Crusades: Eye-
Witness Accounts of the Wars Between Christianity and Islam*,
Weidenfeld and Nicolson, 1989: 3.3B and D
Heritage of Britain, Readers Digest Association, 1975: 3.7B
Jean Marx (Ed.), *Guillaume de Jumieges, Gesta Normannorum
Ducum*, Societé de L'Histoire de Normandie, 1914: 2.2C
T. W. Moody and F. X. Matin (Eds.), *The Course of Irish
History*, Mercier Press, 1967: 3.6A, B and C
Peter Moss, *History Alive*, Hart Davis Educational Ltd, 1977:
3.1A
L. du Garde Peach, *The Kings and Queens of England*, Ladybird
Books, 1968: 3.5A
D. Richards and A. D. Ellis, *Medieval Britain*, Longman, 1973:
3.4A, 3.7A, 5.2A
Schools Council Project: History 13–16, *Medicine Through
Time 2: The Beginning of Change*, Holmes McDougall, 1976:
4.8C, 5.1G
Paul Shuter and John Child, *Skills in History 1: Changes*,
Heinemann Educational, 1987: 1.1B
L. E. Snellgrove, *The Early Modern Age*, Longman, 1972: 4.9B
David Whitehall, *Life in Norman Times*, Edward Arnold,
1989: 2.3A, 2.4A, 3.1C and 4.2C

CONTENTS

PART ONE   INTRODUCTION
1.1   Types of Sources   4

PART TWO   THE NORMAN CONQUEST
2.1   Why was there an Invasion?   6
2.2   The Norman Victory   8
2.3   The Victory Completed   10
2.4   Keeping Control: The Feudal System   12
2.5   Keeping Control: Motte & Bailey Castles   14
2.6   Keeping Control: Square Keep Castles   16
2.7   The Land the Normans Ruled   18

PART THREE   THE MEDIEVAL REALMS TAKE SHAPE
3.1   The Church and Christendom   20
3.2   The Murder of Thomas Becket   22
3.3   The Crusades   24
3.4   Magna Carta   26
3.5   Simon de Montfort, Hero or Villain?   28
3.6   Henry II and Ireland   30
3.7   Edward I and Wales   32
3.8   Robert Bruce and Bannockburn   34

PART FOUR   LIVING IN THE MEDIEVAL REALMS
4.1   Medieval Warfare   36
4.2   Crime and Punishment   38
4.3   Religious Beliefs   40
4.4   Life in a Medieval Monastery   42
4.5   Life in a Medieval Village   44
4.6   Life in a Medieval Town   46
4.7   Women in Medieval Times   48
4.8   Medicine   50
4.9   The Development of the English Language   52

PART FIVE   THE END OF THE MEDIEVAL REALMS?
5.1   The Black Death – the Plague Arrives   54
5.2   The Black Death – Effects   56
5.3   The Peasants' Revolt – Why did it Happen?   58
5.4   The Peasants' Revolt – What Happened?   60
5.5   The Wars of the Roses   62
Index   64

1.1 Types of Sources

In this book you will learn about the events of the years 1066–1500. Historians call this time the **Medieval** period of history, or the **Middle Ages**. But how do they know what happened then? After all, there were no cameras and hardly any books. Indeed it was a time when very few people could read or write.

Piecing together what happened in the past is one of the most exciting things about studying history. It can be a bit like putting together a jigsaw. To do this, historians use **sources**. A source is simply something which can be used to get information about the past. It might be a very detailed book, written by a university professor. It could be nothing more than a tiny piece of pottery which has survived from the time you are studying. These sources can be divided into two types.

Primary sources come from the time that you are studying. They are not based on other sources. Some primary sources are written and some are not. (Historians usually say they are non-written.) **Artefacts** (things people have made) are primary sources. As we are studying the medieval period, Norman castles and cathedrals will be primary sources, and also clothes, pottery or even expensive jewellery from the same time.

Secondary sources usually come from later than the time of the events they are describing. They are based on other sources. Most secondary sources are written, like school textbooks, but they can also be non-written. If you made a model of a Norman castle in your class, then it would be a secondary source.

Some sources which come from the medieval period are shown on these pages. They will help you understand the different types of sources historians use.

B **A description of William Rufus.**

SOURCE

He was very harsh and fierce in his rule. To his followers and all his neighbours he was very frightening. Everything that was hateful to God and to good men was the daily practice in this land during his reign. Therefore he was hated by almost all his people.

Written by a monk during the reign of William Rufus, 1087–1100.

C

SOURCE

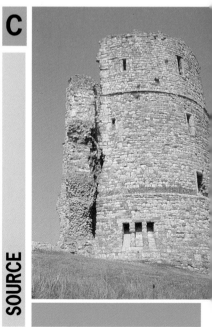

Hadleigh Castle in Essex, built in 1232.

A

SOURCE

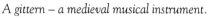

A gittern – a medieval musical instrument.

A scene from the Bayeux Tapestry (made in about 1080) showing fighting between the Normans and the English.

Activities...

1 Historians use both primary and secondary sources. What are the differences between them?

2 Copy the following chart:

Type	Source
Primary written	
Primary non-written	
Building	
Artefact	
Secondary	

Now look carefully at Sources A–E and decide how you would describe each source. Fill in the source letters against the description you think is correct. Some sources may fit more than one description

3 Which source do you think contains:
   a the most information?
   b the most interesting information?
   c the most important information?
   In each case explain your answer carefully.

4 The monk in Source B was writing during the reign of William Rufus. Do you think an historian today would write the same things about him? Explain your answer carefully.

A modern school textbook on the medieval period, published in 1991.

2.1 Why was there an Invasion?

At the beginning of 1066, England was ruled by King Edward. He was a very religious man who spent so much time praying and confessing his sins that his people called him Edward 'the Confessor'. He was old and very sick. People thought he would not live much longer.

Edward had no children and his only nephew, Edgar, was far too young to become king. So Edward chose as his successor **Harold Godwinson**, the Earl of Wessex. Harold was the most powerful English noble and leader of the army. Also, Edward was married to Harold's sister. So the choice was not surprising. The nobles agreed with it too. Harold was a strong leader who would make sure that the nobles kept their positions of power. When Edward died on 5 January 1066, the nobles met in their council, called the **Witan**, and agreed that Harold should be king. He was crowned Harold II on the day that Edward was buried.

Not everyone was happy with the choice. **King Harald Hardrada** of Norway thought that he should have the English throne. One of his ancestors, King Cnut, had ruled England and Hardrada thought this meant that he should now be king. He knew that England was a rich country, and that lots of taxes could be collected. Hardrada was already a very powerful king with a large army and he also had the support of Tostig, Harold Godwinson's brother. Tostig had fallen out with Godwinson and supported Hardrada to get revenge.

There was an even more serious opponent for Harold Godwinson much nearer home. This was **Duke William of Normandy**. Edward the Confessor had been brought up in Normandy and had many Norman advisors in his court. In 1051, William visited Edward. William claimed that during this visit, Edward promised to name him as his successor. Many people believed William's claim.

NORWAY

ENGLAND

NORMANDY

William also thought that Harold Godwinson could not become King of England because of an oath that he had taken. In 1064, Harold had been captured on a visit to Normandy and taken to William. William made Harold take an oath promising to help him become King of England. This event is shown on the Bayeux Tapestry (see Source A). Of course Harold was probably forced to agree to what William wanted, but this did not stop William from calling him an 'oath-breaker'. Oath-breaking was a very serious thing to be accused of. This meant that William got support to invade England from the Pope, Alexander II. The Pope gave William a special banner – and William said his attack on England would be a 'holy crusade'.

William had other reasons, too, for attacking England. In Normandy he was just a Duke, but in England he would be a king. This sounded much more important. He also knew that his followers in Normandy needed rewards to stay loyal to him. England was larger and richer than Normandy. What better way to reward them than to give them large estates in conquered England?

Harold Godwinson had inherited a fiercely disputed kingdom.

Activities...

1 When Edward died, why was it difficult to decide who would be king?

2 **a** Which three men wanted to be king after Edward?
   b Explain why each of them thought that they should be king.

3 Does Source A **prove** that Harold swore an oath to help William become the next king of England?

4 Who do you think should have been king after Edward? Give reasons for your answer.

Harold Godwinson swearing an oath to Duke William, from the Bayeux Tapestry.

A

SOURCE

2.2 The Norman Victory

Early in 1066 people saw a 'long-haired' star in the sky. This was **Halley's comet** which appears over England every 75 years. People at this time were superstitious and many of them believed that the star was a sign from God. They thought something terrible was about to happen. By the end of the year they had been proved right. There had been two invasions and two kings had been killed.

One invasion came from Duke William of Normandy. He spent much of the summer of 1066 preparing his forces. King Harold tried to block any invasion by William by placing his army and his fleet on the south coast.

By August William was ready to invade, but could not leave Normandy as the winds were against him. This gave Harold time to organize, but by September his army was running out of food. Also, he had to send many of his soldiers home where they were needed to collect the harvest. Shortly afterwards many of his ships were destroyed by gales in the Channel. There now seemed little to stop William.

But it was Harold's other great opponent who struck first. On 18 September, Hardrada led a huge invasion fleet up the River Humber. Tostig, Harold's treacherous brother, was with him. On 20 September, they defeated the English forces at the **Battle of Fulford**. Harold had to collect his soldiers and march north to fight Hardrada.

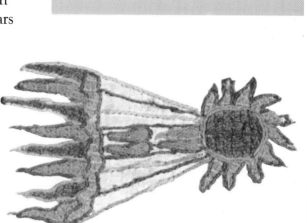

Halley's comet, as shown on the Bayeux Tapestry.

York • ✕ • Stamford Bridge
✕
Fulford •
R. Humber

NORTH S

Hardrada and Tostig land with invasion fleet

ENGLAND

Harold marches north to face Hardrada

Harold marches south to face William

R. Thames
• London

Pevensey • ✕ Hastings

William lands at Pevensey

ENGLISH CHANNEL

• St Val

NORMANDY

Bayeux •

— Hardrada

— Harold

— William

After marching nearly 200 miles, Harold won a great victory at the **Battle of Stamford Bridge**. Hardrada and Tostig were among the thousands killed and the survivors needed only 24 boats to sail home. They had arrived in 300! Unfortunately for Harold, while he was in the north, the wind in the Channel changed. William crossed from Normandy with no one to stop him. Once more Harold was forced to carry out an exhausting march – this time of over 250 miles. On the night of 13 October he arrived at Hastings.

The following morning Harold placed his troops, mostly foot soldiers, along the ridge of a hill near Hastings. His best men were at the front. These were **housecarls** who were said to be able to cut off a horse's head with a single blow of their two-handed axes! William's forces contained large numbers of mounted knights but they were at a disadvantage because they had to charge uphill at the English.

When the **Battle of Hastings** started, the fighting was fierce and lasted almost until nightfall. Norman archers fired a constant stream of arrows into the English 'shield wall', but still it stood firm. The Normans finally broke the English forces with a series of attacks and trick retreats. Thinking the Normans were running away, the English chased them – only to be cut down when the Norman knights turned and attacked. Victory came at last to the Normans when Harold was killed (Source C).

C **SOURCE**

Harold himself, fighting at the front of his army, fell covered with deadly wounds. The English, seeing their king dead, lost confidence in their own safety, and as night was approaching they turned and fled.

A Norman monk, William of Jumieges, writing in 1070.

Activities...

1   **a** Why do you think people in 1066 were so concerned about the 'long-haired' star?
    b Do you think a modern historian would put details about comets in a description of wars and invasions? Explain your answer carefully.

2   What can an historian studying the events of 1066 learn from Source B?

3   'We cannot believe what Source C says because it was written by a Norman'. Explain whether you agree or disagree with this statement.

4   Suppose that you had just 30 seconds to tell the story of 1066. What would you say?

B **SOURCE**

Part of the Bayeux Tapestry, showing the Normans preparing for the invasion.

2.3 The Victory Completed

William had defeated the English army, but not all of the English nobles fought at Hastings. They might still try to oppose him. As he was not sure what the English would do, William did not march to London. First, he captured the castle at Dover, then the cities of Canterbury and Winchester, the old capital.

In December, William marched on to London. He showed how powerful he was by burning down property and killing the English. Soon the English nobles told him that they would accept him as king. He was crowned at Westminster Abbey on Christmas Day, 1066.

To establish control, William made the English nobles swear an oath of loyalty to him. If they did this they were allowed to keep their lands, although much of England was given to men who had fought for William at Hastings. The English did not always accept their new Norman lords without a fight – especially when taxes were put up. In 1067, there was a rebellion in Kent and in the next year a more serious one in Exeter. Both were soon put down.

By far the most important rebellion took place in the North. With the help of a large force sent by the King of Denmark, English rebels burnt William's castle in York to the ground. Once he had defeated the rebels, William decided to teach them a lesson. He destroyed villages and farms across a wide area, and slaughtered livestock. This **Harrying of the North** caused terrible famine and many people died of starvation.

There was more resistance to William, centred around Ely in the low-lying Fens. The rebels used their knowledge of the area to hide on islands in the marshes. It was not until 1071 that the Normans found a way into the marshes and put down the revolt.

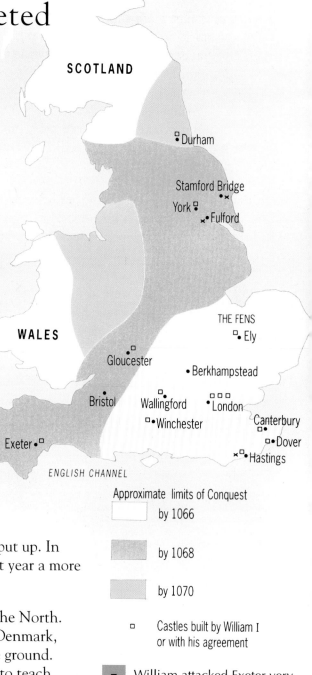

Approximate limits of Conquest

☐ by 1066

▨ by 1068

▨ by 1070

□ Castles built by William I or with his agreement

A William attacked Exeter very fiercely because one of the Englishmen standing on the castle wall bared his bottom and broke wind in front of the Normans.

SOURCE

Account by the English monk William of Malmesbury, written in 1120.

The rebel leader Earl Hereward 'the Wake' managed to escape and many romantic stories exist about what happened to him. Yet historians have never found any further records of this last great English opponent of the Normans.

By the early 1070s the conquest of England was complete. Now William had to make sure that the conquest would be a long-lasting one.

B

SOURCE

People were so hungry that they ate human flesh as well as horses, cats and dogs. It was horrific to see human corpses decaying in the houses and roads, and there was a terrible smell because there was no one alive to bury them. For nine years no one lived in the villages between York and Durham.

An English monk, writing early in the 12th century, describes the results of the 'Harrying of the North'.

A 19th-century painting showing Hereward attacking the Normans.

C

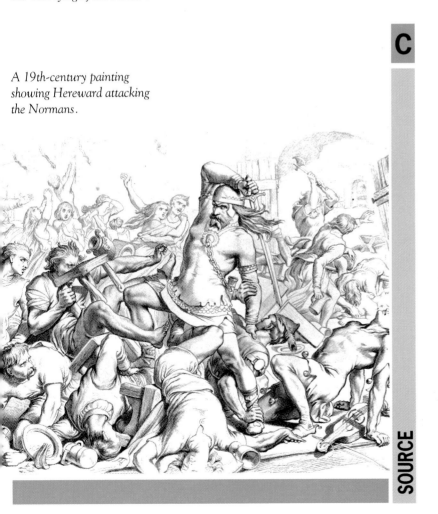

SOURCE

Activities...

1 Here are four statements about Duke William.
- As soon as he had won at Hastings, William marched to London.
- On his way to London, William burned down property and killed some of the English.
- The English nobles told William that they did not want him to be king.
- William was crowned on Christmas Day, 1066.

Two of these statements are true and two are false.
   a Write all four statements in your book, and correct the false ones.

2 Source A tells us why William was harsh on Exeter. Do you think that this was the real reason for his harshness? Explain your answer.

3 The English said that the 'Harrying of the North' was mean and cruel. The Normans said it showed William was strong and brave.
   a Write an entry in a Chronicle by a Saxon reporting the 'Harrying of the North'.
   b Explain how a report written by a Norman might be different.

4 If we didn't have Source C we would not know what Hereward the Wake looks like.' Do you agree?

2.4 Keeping Control: The Feudal System

Once William had become King of England, he had to decide how he was going to govern the country. He didn't want the old English nobles to keep their estates, because they would be too powerful and might try to overthrow him. Anyway, they had to make room for William's supporters who had been promised land in return for helping him.

William was very careful not to just give land away. His supporters were rewarded, but they had duties to perform as well. This system of duties and rewards was called the **Feudal System**. In Normandy when barons or bishops were given land they had to swear an oath of loyalty to the lord who was giving it. This was called **doing homage**. The barons or bishops then became **tenants-in-chief** and agreed to provide knights (mounted soldiers) to guard castles or fight in wars for their lords. The more land the baron was given, the more knights he had to provide.

The tenants-in-chief sometimes had their knights living with them in their castles. Usually, however, they gave some of their own land to the knights, who in return did homage and agreed to fight when asked. The knights became **under-tenants**. They kept some land for themselves and shared the rest among the **peasants** who farmed it. The peasants did homage to the knights who, in turn, promised to protect them.

The feudal system proved ideal for distributing the land of newly-conquered England. William could have a large army whenever he liked, without the expense of keeping soldiers at his royal court. He also made sure that his supporters were rewarded, and at the same time stayed loyal to him.

The oath taken in Norman times when doing homage.

A 13th-century painting showing a knight doing homage to the king.

How the feudal system worked.

Activities...

1 Copy this passage into your book, filling in the gaps.

   William did not want the _____ nobles to keep their land. He wanted to give it to his _____ As well as receiving land, the nobles had to swear an _____ and agree to do _____. William needed an army so the nobles had to promise to provide _____ for him.
   The nobles already knew about this system because it was used in _____. It was called the _____ system.

2 Explain what the following were in Norman England:
   a a tenant-in-chief
   b an under-tenant
   c doing homage
   d knights.

3 Imagine that you were able to carry out a radio interview with the following people:
   a an English noble
   b a Norman baron
   c an English peasant.

   Your first question to them is 'Do you think that the feudal system is fair?'
   What do you think each person would say?

2.5 Keeping Control: Motte & Bailey Castles

The Normans had taken control of England by force. Many English people hated them and would have attacked them if they had been given a chance. Castles were a way of keeping the Normans and their followers safe. The Norman lords built them wherever they settled. William made sure that castles were built in the major towns, so that there would always be Normans to keep the town loyal.

The earliest castles were built very quickly – sometimes in just a few days. At first the Normans used earth and wood because these materials were easily available and quick to use. The early castles were known as **motte and bailey castles** because they had two main features. A large mound of earth (called the **motte**) was constructed and a wooden tower was built on top. From this, the soldiers could see all the surrounding land in case of attack. It also meant the English people saw the castle wherever they went – so they were always reminded of the strength of the Normans.

Beside the motte was the **bailey**. This was a large yard, with a ditch and fence around the outside. The soldiers lived here – they occupied the wooden tower on the motte only when the castle was being attacked. Animals and food were also stored in the bailey.

It was very important to build the castles near major routes. This made it easier for the Norman soldiers to move quickly, and to block the movements of an enemy army. In this way, they kept control over all the countryside within 20–30 miles of the castle. If the castle could be made harder to attack by building it on a hill or next to a river, so much the better.

During William's reign, more than 60 of these castles were built all over England. They helped to make sure that William's conquest would be safe. The remains of motte and bailey castles can still be seen in some places today, but the wooden keeps have not survived.

A **SOURCE**

Carisbrooke Castle.

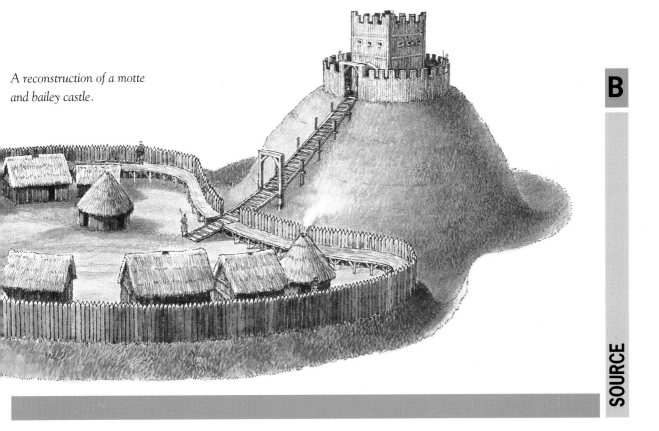

A reconstruction of a motte and bailey castle.

B

SOURCE

SOURCE

C

The remains of the motte and bailey castle at Pleshey in Essex. The motte and the bailey can be clearly seen.

Activities...

1   **a** Why did the Normans build castles?
    b How did they decide where to build them?

2   You are an English noble living near a newly-constructed motte and bailey castle. A fellow noble in another part of the country has just written to you asking what this castle is like. Write back to him describing the castle.

3   Why is it difficult for historians to know exactly what motte and bailey castles looked like?

4   Motte and bailey castles were designed to resist attack. Can you think of the best way of attacking them?

2.6 Keeping Control: Square Keep Castles

Motte and bailey castles had weaknesses. They were built out of wood, which rotted easily and could be set on fire by enemy soldiers. They were also cramped, drafty and uncomfortable. Since the beginning of the conquest the Normans had built some important castles, like the White Tower in London, out of stone. After 1100, many more stone castles were built and they were usually square in shape.

The square stone keeps were very strong. The walls were up to 4 metres thick. Because the stone was so heavy, it was not possible to build the keep on top of a motte. Therefore, the doorway of the keep was usually built on the first floor, making it harder for attackers to reach. The windows on the lower floors were just thin slits – wide enough to fire an arrow out, but too narrow to let an attacker in. There were a variety of rooms. Some were used for storage of food or weapons and some, like the Great Hall, were used for eating and sleeping. With their narrow windows and large stone rooms, they must have been dark and draughty places to live!

It took a very strong army to force its way in to one of these castles. Square keeps were very hard to knock down or burn, so the attackers usually had to try to starve the defenders out. As time went on, more and more improvements were made to make the castles even stronger. The castles were such strong bases for soldiers that the Normans began to conquer Scotland and Wales. They built chains of castles to control the hostile people of those areas.

The square keep of Rochester Castle which was begun in 1127 by Henry I.

A

SOURCE

The lord and his family lived in the keep all of the time. It could be used by everyone in the castle as a last stronghold if they were under attack. It would have been very cramped with everyone inside.

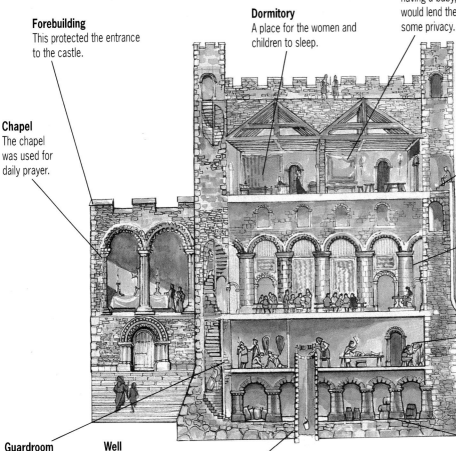

Forebuilding
This protected the entrance to the castle.

Chapel
The chapel was used for daily prayer.

Dormitory
A place for the women and children to sleep.

Lord's room
The only room where the lord and his family could be private. If someone was ill, or having a baby, then the lord would lend them his room for some privacy.

Toilets
The toilets were set above each other, and had a central drain which opened on the outside of the keep. The drains were kept small, so that the attackers could not get in that way.

Great Hall
The largest and most important room in the keep. It was used by everyone for eating and meeting together.

Kitchen
The kitchen was used for very basic cooking. Most keeps had bigger kitchens in the bailey.

Cellars
Food, arms and ammunition were stored in the cellars. Prisoners were kept here, too.

Guardroom
The guardroom was used by off-duty guards.

Well
Keeps were deliberately built in places where there was water for a well, otherwise the defenders could easily have been starved out.

Activities...

1 Below is a list of possible reasons why the Normans built square keep castles:
   - They were frightened of the English.
   - They wanted to show how powerful they were.
   - Motte and bailey castles were not good enough.
   - They wanted somewhere comfortable to live.

   a Do you think that any of these is **not** a reason why the Normans built square keep castles? Give reasons for your answer.

   b Explain why each of the others is a possible reason why they built them.

2 Why were stone square keep castles so hard to attack?

3 If you want to know what a castle looked like when it was built, why should you be careful about using the remains that exist today?

2.7 The Land the Normans Ruled

By 1086, William ruled throughout England. He was concerned that his new kingdom might be attacked from abroad, and wanted to bring more soldiers from France for protection. Could he get more taxes from the English to pay for this? William did not know. In fact he did not really know much about how wealthy England was. So he decided to find out.

In 1086, he sent officials into the parishes of England to carry out an enormous survey. When they had finished asking their questions, a second group of officials was sent to each parish to check that the villagers had been telling the truth. No wonder it became known as the **Domesday Survey**. Domesday is the Day of Judgement – no one can escape that, and no one seemed to be able to escape William's survey.

Although no such survey had ever been done before, William's officials completed their task in just under a year. It was a tremendous achievement, and it told William just what he wanted to know. Many people were much richer than he had realized. Now he could make them pay the correct amount of tax.

The information which was collected was written up in two volumes, **Great Domesday** and **Little Domesday**. These have survived to the present day and are very useful to historians. (Although there are no records for some parts of the country.) Some of the most interesting information concerns every-day life in England, that we would otherwise know little about. We are told about female slaves in the county of Herefordshire, and rents paid in eels in Wiltshire – even that there was an overgrown garden in Somerset. William's survey was so detailed that 900 years later we can still read about how a woman called Aelfgyth was given a small plot of land by a local landowner on condition that she 'taught his daughter how to embroider'.

A **SOURCE**

William wanted to know what taxes were owed to him. The enquiry was very thorough. There was not a single yard of land and not even – it is shameful to record – one ox, cow or pig that was not recorded.

From 'The Anglo-Saxon Chronicle', an account of yearly events recorded by English monks.

In Shipley, Ravenchil owned one hide of land in Edward's reign. There was room for two ploughs and it was worth 10 shillings a year. Now it is wasteland. Robert de Lacey owns it.
(One hide is enough to keep one family – this was usually about 120 acres.)

The Domesday entry for the village of Shipley in Yorkshire.

Activities...

1 **a** Why did William's survey become known as the 'Domesday' survey?
   b Why was William so keen to carry out the survey?
   c How accurate do you think the survey was? Give reasons for your answer.

2 Why do you think the *Anglo-Saxon Chronicle* described William's survey as 'shameful?'

3 Source B tells us about the village of Shipley in 1086.
   a What is interesting about the name of the owner, Robert de Lacey?
   b Can you think of any reason why Shipley is described as 'wasteland' at this time?

4 Copy the diagram below into your book. Explain what it tells you about England in 1086.

Types of people living in England in 1086

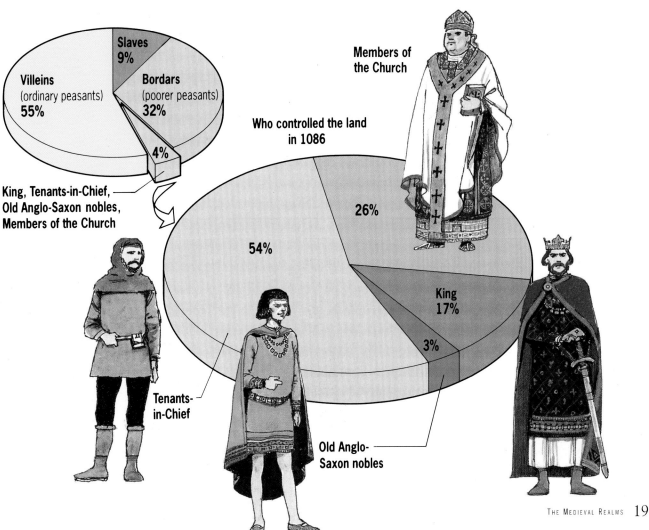

Villeins (ordinary peasants) 55%

Slaves 9%

Bordars (poorer peasants) 32%

4%

King, Tenants-in-Chief, Old Anglo-Saxon nobles, Members of the Church

Who controlled the land in 1086

Members of the Church

26%

54%

King 17%

3%

Tenants-in-Chief

Old Anglo-Saxon nobles

The Church and Christendom

The spread of Christianity

Christianity first came to Britain when it was part of the Roman Empire. When the Romans left, many Christians went back to worshipping their old gods. But there were some Christians left in Britain, particularly in Wales and Ireland. They worked to convert the British people back to Christianity. The Pope also sent missionaries from Rome to try to make the British Christian again.

By the beginning of the medieval period Britain was fully Christian once more. It was part of **Christendom**. This means that it saw itself as part of the Christian community in the wider world. It was a bit like being in a club together. All Christians believed that the Pope was head of the Church.

Of course when we say 'Church' we don't mean the building where you say your prayers! Head of the Church meant being in charge of the whole organization responsible for looking after religion. Today we have many different types of Christian Church (like the Church of England or the Methodist Church). In medieval times the Church was called the 'Catholic' church, because Catholic meant everyone belonged to it.

A

SOURCE

As the Pope was God's representative on earth, everyone – princes, kings and emperors were subject to him. In the interests of the Church as a whole, the Pope could order one king to invade and conquer another's country.
A king who defied or offended the Pope could be excommunicated – that is expelled from the Church. As he was no longer a Christian his subjects need not obey him and were entitled to rebel.

The importance of the Pope. From 'History Alive' by Peter Moss, 1977.

People who had important jobs in the Church often helped the king run the country. For example, Bishop Roger of Salisbury was one of King Henry I's best government officials. Of course bishops and abbots were also important because they controlled large areas of land, and this made them wealthy and powerful. So kings tried to make sure that only people they could trust became abbots or bishops. But this was not always easy. Sometimes the Pope did not agree with the king about who should have the top jobs in the Church.

During the reign of William the Conqueror there was no problem. He was a very religious man who founded several abbeys, including one on the site where the Battle of Hastings had taken place. William appointed **Lanfranc**, an abbot from Normandy, as **Archbishop of Canterbury**. This was the most important job in the English Church. Lanfranc said that priests must not marry and made sure that monks stuck more closely to their vows. The Pope agreed with these measures. But William also cleverly increased his own control over the Church. All the English bishops and priests were replaced by Norman ones who were guaranteed to support him.

William Rufus, who was king after the Conqueror, was not such a religious man. When Lanfranc died in 1089, the king didn't bother to appoint a new Archbishop for four years. Then William quarelled with the new Archbishop, who was called Anselm. In the end Anselm left the country and did not return until William's death in 1100.

Anselm also argued with the next king, Henry I. This time the dispute was over who should choose new bishops and abbots. Henry thought he should decide, but the Pope and Anselm said it was their right, not Henry's. Neither Henry nor the Pope really wanted to quarrel, so they patched up their differences. But the next disagreement between a king and the Pope proved to be much more serious.

B

SOURCE

Tell the Archbishop that I hated him yesterday, and I hate him more today, and I shall hate him even more tomorrow.

A message sent to Anselm by William Rufus.

C

SOURCE

Then he sent for some knights who came into the abbey fully armed. Some of the monks went into the church and locked the doors. But the knights broke in. They killed three monks and wounded eighteen in the church. Their blood flowed from the altar onto the steps, and from the steps onto the floor.

How the abbot of Glastonbury dealt with monks who would not sing Norman prayers.

Activities...

1 Explain what each of these words mean:
   a missionary
   b Christendom
   c the Church
   d catholic.

2 Read Source A. Why do you think kings in medieval times were so keen to be on good terms with the Pope?

3 Why were medieval kings so bothered about who had the best jobs in the Church?

4 a What does Source B tell you about what sort of person William Rufus was?
   b What does Source C tell you about what sort of person the abbot of Glastonbury was?

3.2 The Murder of Thomas Becket

On 29 December 1170, the Archbishop of Canterbury, Thomas Becket, was murdered in Canterbury Cathedral. The four knights who carried out the murder claimed that they were acting on orders from the king. How could such a terrible thing have happened?

Becket had been appointed Archbishop by Henry II, in 1162. He and Henry had been friends for many years and the king expected that the new Archbishop would support him in everything he did. But Becket had strong views on the importance of the Church.

Medieval priests did not always behave as we would expect our priests today to behave. Some of them committed crimes and had to be punished. But these priests could ask to be tried by the Church's own courts and often got light sentences. Henry did not like this, and passed new laws saying that priests should be tried in the king's courts like everyone else. Becket said Henry was interfering with the rights of the Church. He and Henry quarrelled so strongly that, in 1165, Becket left England.

Becket returned in 1170 and he and Henry tried to work together. But Becket was so cross about what had happened he immediately **excommunicated** (expelled from the Church) all those bishops who had been helping Henry while he was abroad. The king could hardly believe it. In his anger he is said to have shouted: 'Will no one rid me of this turbulent priest?' Four knights decided that Henry wanted Becket dead and murdered him. Henry later claimed that he had not meant that at all.

Soon people began to believe that miracles were happening at the spot where Becket died. The Pope announced that Becket would be called a saint and people came from far and wide to pray at the tomb of St Thomas, 'God's holy martyr'.

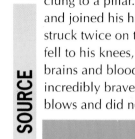

A They pulled and dragged him. They wanted to get him outside the church to kill him, but he clung to a pillar. He bowed his head in prayer and joined his hands together. He was then struck twice on the head. At the third blow he fell to his knees, and the fourth blow spilt his brains and blood on the floor. He was incredibly brave. He did not try to stop the blows and did not cry out.

SOURCE

The death of Becket as described by his assistant, Edward Grim. It is probably Grim who is standing by the altar in Source B.

B

SOURCE

An illustration of Becket's murder drawn in about 1200.

C SOURCE

The murder of Becket as shown in about 1325. (This illustration has been deliberately defaced – probably in the 16th century).

D SOURCE

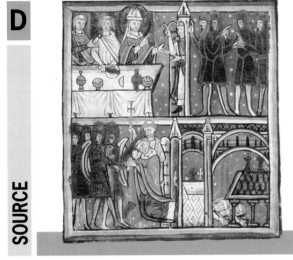

An illustration from 1180. It shows the four knights arriving while Becket sits at supper. They kill him and later pray at his shrine.

E SOURCE

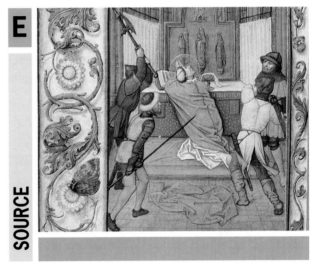

A Dutch illustration of Becket's murder. Painted in about 1480.

Activities...

1 Why did the four knights murder Becket?

2 The Pope said that Becket was a saint. Do you think that Henry would have agreed? Explain your answer carefully.

3 Sources B, C, D and E are illustrations of Becket's death from the medieval period.
   a In what ways do these sources agree with what Edward Grim said in Source A?

   b In what ways do they disagree?
   c What is the difference between the soldiers in Source B and those in Source E?
   d Can you explain why there is a difference between them?
   e Does the fact that the soldiers in Source E are different mean that Source E is not a reliable piece of evidence for the historian? Explain your answer carefully.

3.3 The Crusades

By the beginning of the Middle Ages much of Europe was Christian. However, the land where Jesus lived and was crucified (the **Holy Land**) was controlled by **Muslims** – people who followed the teaching of the prophet Muhammed.

Until 1095, the Muslims allowed Christians to visit the Holy Land and thousands of pilgrims travelled to Jerusalem to see where Jesus died and was buried. But in 1095, the Holy Land was captured by Muslims from Turkey. They would not allow Christian pilgrims to visit and killed many of those who ignored their instructions.

So in 1096, **Pope Urban II** asked the Christian leaders of Europe to launch a **Crusade** (a holy war) to win back Jerusalem for the Christian faith. Those people who went to the Holy Land to fight were called crusaders and carried banners with a red cross on a white background to show that they were fighting for Christ.

Christians from all over Europe went to fight in the Crusades. Many crusaders genuinely wanted to capture Jerusalem, but they also had other reasons. Some thought that fighting in a Crusade was a good way to be forgiven for their sins. For others, it provided a chance to win land or to control the rich trade in spices and silk that came from this area. There were even some kings who were glad to get rid of troublesome knights for a while!

Between 1096 and 1270 there were seven different Crusades. Relations between muslims and christians became very bitter. During this time many tragic incidents occurred, but perhaps none is sadder than the **Children's Crusade** of 1212 (see Source A). One of the leaders of the **Third Crusade** was Richard I of England. His bravery in battles with the Muslim leader, Saladin, earned him the title 'Lionheart'. But eventually he was forced to make peace with Saladin and return home.

Although Jerusalem was captured several times it was always won back by the Muslims. In 1291, Acre, the last Christian city in the Holy Land, was captured by the Muslims. The Christians of Europe were forced to accept that the Holy Land would remain in Muslim hands.

A **SOURCE**

In 1212 two armies of children, one from France and one from Germany, set out to recapture Jerusalem. Their faith was so strong that they were convinced that the Mediterranean Sea would dry up in front of them, like the Red Sea had dried up in front of the Israelites. This crusade ended disastrously with almost all of the children either drowned in the sea or starved to death or sold into slavery in Africa.

From 'The Pursuit of the Millennium' by N. Cohn, 1970.

B **SOURCE**

I will tell you about Saladin, that great persecutor of christianity. When he worked for Nur ad-Din of Damascus he earned a disgraceful income from running brothels. He also devoted much of his time to taverns and gaming. When he became ruler he took over surrounding countries either by force or trickery. This greedy tyrant, not satisfied with these possessions, concentrated all of his efforts on seizing the Holy Land.

From a Chronicle about Richard I, written by a monk in London in the early 13th century.

The siege of Jerusalem, 1099. From a French 14th-century manuscript.

Saladin was so determined to fight the holy war that he thought of nothing else. From the time that he decided to fight, he never spent a single gold coin on anything else. He also made sure that his men were fed and cared for properly when they were ill. So pure was his character that he would not allow a bad word to be said about anyone, preferring to hear only about their good points.

From a description of Saladin by Baha ad-Din Ibn Shaddad, a muslim historian who lived at Saladin's court.

Activities...

1 a Why did it become necessary to launch the Crusades?
   b Why did so many Christians support the Crusades?

2 What does Source A tell you about the beliefs of people at the time?

3 What methods of attack are being used in Source C?

4 Source C was painted during the 14th century, but the siege of Jerusalem was in 1099. Does this mean historians will not find Source C a useful source?

5 a What did the author of Source B think about Saladin?
   b What did the author of Source D think about Saladin?
   c Why do you think these sources disagree?
   d Does this mean one of them must be lying?

3.4 Magna Carta

A

SOURCE

He would gnash his teeth and roll his staring eyes in fury. Then he would pick up sticks and straws and gnaw them like a lunatic.

King John's temper described by a monk writing shortly after John's death in 1216.

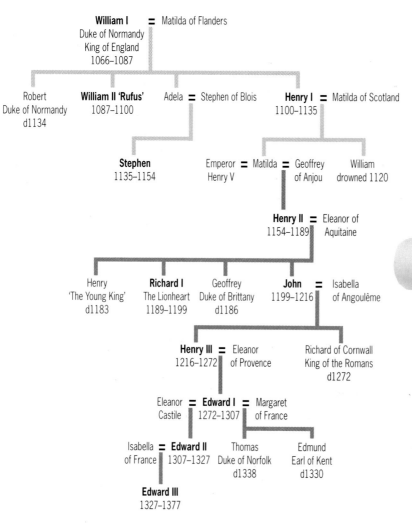

The Kings of England 1066–1377.

Magna Carta

I, King John, accept that I have to govern according to the law.

So I agree:

1 Not to imprison nobles without trial

2 That trials must be in courts; not held in secret by me

3 To have fair taxation for the nobles

4 To let freemen travel wherever they like

5 Not to interfere in Church matters

6 Not to seize crops without paying for them

. . . and lot more things too!

John has sometimes been called 'the worst ever King of England'. But in some ways he was unlucky. John's father, Henry II, had built up a large empire in France. His brother, Richard the Lionheart, won glory in the Crusades. But John was a poor soldier and allowed the King of France to take back most of the land that England owned there. The people of England liked their kings to be great warriors. So John was unpopular.

John tried to win back the land, but was unsuccessful. The fighting was expensive and taxes were higher than they had ever been before. People complained bitterly. John even fell out with the Pope over who should be Archbishop of Canterbury.

Finally, in 1214, a group of powerful barons drew up a list of complaints. They told John he was ruling unfairly. When he refused to change, they raised an army and captured London. Now John had to listen. On 15 June 1215, he met the barons at **Runnymede**, a meadow beside the river Thames, and agreed to sign the **Magna Carta** or Great Charter. A special council of 25 barons was set up to make sure John kept his word.

Although John later tried to back out of the agreement, Magna Carta was here to stay. Every king for the next 250 years agreed to rule by it. Of course, many of them broke the terms of Magna Carta from time to time. There was still injustice, and kings still argued with barons and with the Church. But the important thing was that they knew that their people expected them to rule according to the law.

Soon the people began to help more in running the country. From 1295, kings began to call bishops, noblemen and wealthy people from the towns and countryside to meet in a **Parliament** in London. At first it just gave the king advice, but gradually Parliament became more and more important. In time it was Parliament, not the king, which ruled the country.

Activities...

1. Using the information on these pages draw a timeline of the kings of England from 1066 to 1216. Don't forget to include their dates.

2. Source A describes King John as behaving 'like a lunatic'. Is there any reason why we should doubt what it says? Explain your answer.

3. **a** List six things King John agreed to in the Magna Carta.
   b Which of those six things would have helped:
   - a noble
   - a bishop
   - a peasant?

4. 'The nobles made King John sign the Magna Carta because he was a bad king and he was ruling badly'. Explain whether you agree or disagree with this statement.

5. Some historians have said that Magna Carta is the most important document in our history. What do you think they mean by this?

B

SOURCE

King John with the Magna Carta. From an embroidery made in 1966.

3.5 Simon de Montfort, Hero or Villain?

Simon de Montfort was born in France in 1208. His father was one of the great nobles of his time and a successful general. King Henry III of England was well-known for favouring foreigners. In 1229, de Montfort came to England and immediately became one of the king's favourites. In 1231, Henry made him Earl of Leicester and in 1238 de Montfort married Henry's sister. Later, de Montfort became one of Henry's most determined enemies. He led a revolt of English barons against the king between 1258 and 1265. For a short time de Montfort was the real ruler of England, but this did not last. In 1265 he was killed, and his army defeated by the king's, at the **Battle of Evesham.**

There were many barons who rebelled against their king between 1066 and 1500. Simon de Montfort is famous, however, because during his rebellion he is supposed to have called the first real **Parliament**. The material in this Unit will help you answer two questions. Was Simon de Montfort the inventor of Parliament, and, why did he do the things he did?

A

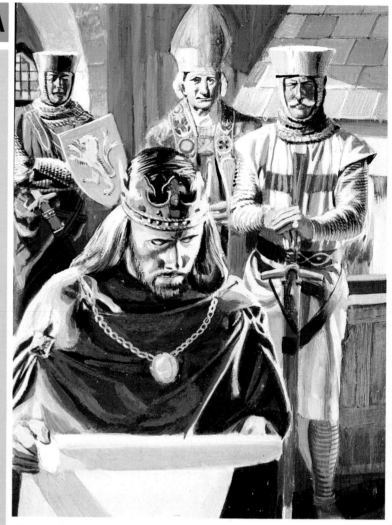

Simon de Montfort forces the captive King Henry III to summon England's first real Parliament.

Henry III proved to be a weak king. He was pious and vain, and the people hated and despised him. He allowed himself to be governed by the foreign relations of his wife, and finally the barons revolted. The foreigners were driven out, and a Parliament of Englishmen summoned to govern the country.

This Parliament is important because it is the first in which ordinary men were allowed to take part. It was summoned by a man named Simon de Montfort, and he not only summoned two knights from each shire, but also two citizens from each town.

SOURCE

From 'The Kings and Queens of England', Ladybird Books, 1968.

Great Councils and Parliaments

The idea of a Parliament, where the king, the lords, and the commons were always represented, grew slowly in the 13th century. Medieval English kings often summoned the most important nobles in the country together. These meetings, called **Great Councils**, advised the king about important decisions and agreed to taxes. Sometimes people called these meetings Parliaments.

A **Parliament** had three sections:
the king, the lords, and the commons. The men summoned to Great Councils were the same men who were lords in a parliament. Representatives of the common people, however, did not usually attend a Great Council.

Here are a few significant events in the development of parliament. Between each of these events, normal Great Councils with just the nobles were often called.

1213 King John summoned a Great Council which included four men from each shire as well as nobles.

1254 Henry III called a meeting of clergy and knights from the various shires. This meeting agreed to taxes.

1265 Simon de Montfort summoned a council with nobles, knights from each shire, and men from selected towns. This is often called the first Parliament.

1272-1294 Edward I called many councils. Sometimes he summoned only nobles. Sometimes he summoned nobles and knights from the shires. Sometimes he summoned nobles, knights from the shires, and men from the towns.

1295 the **Model Parliament** Edward I summoned a parliament with Lords and Commons. The commons were made up from knights chosen from each shire and men from the main towns. This is called the model parliament because, from then on, this was the pattern which was followed.

Simon de Montfort

1248 made Governor of Gascony (part of France, ruled by Henry III).

1252 recalled to England for an investigation into his treatment of the Gascons. De Montfort was found to be innocent, but he resigned angrily because he felt Henry III had not supported him properly.

1258 Main leader of the barons at two Great Councils where it was agreed that Henry III had not been ruling properly and that there should be reforms. These reforms meant Henry had to share power with de Montfort and the other great nobles.

1261 Henry III got the Pope's support to break the reform agreement. At a Great Council, de Montfort felt he was not supported by the other nobles against the king, and he left the country.

1263 A group of nobles on the border between England and Wales fell out with Henry III, demanded the reforms of **1258** again, and called de Montfort back to England to be their leader.

1264 Battle of Lewes. Henry III was defeated by de Montfort and his rebels. England governed by three 'Electors' of whom de Montfort was the most powerful. He summoned a Great Council with no commoners.

1265 De Montfort summoned a second Great Council, this time with commoners as well as lords. In August de Montfort was defeated and killed at the Battle of Evesham.

Activities...

1 Make two timelines. On one show the events in the life of Simon de Montfort, and on the other the events in the development of parliament between 1200 and 1300.

2 What impression of Simon de Montfort do you get from Source A?

3 Are there any statements in Source A you disagree with? For each one copy out the statement and then explain why you disagree with it.

4 One historian called Simon de Montfort 'the only good baron in English history'. Others think he was mainly concerned with looking after himself. Do you think he was a hero we should all look up to?

3.6 Henry II and Ireland

When the Normans first came to England they showed no interest in Ireland. Yet it was a country which would have been easy to conquer. Its armies were weak after years of fighting the Norsemen of Scandanavia, and its people were not united. Instead, it had many kings who fought among themselves for the title of **High King**. Because Ireland was poor, the Normans could not see any advantage in trying to take it over.

Although William Rufus talked about invading Ireland, he never did. Ireland was largely ignored by the Norman kings, until the reign of Henry II. In 1155 the Pope, who was worried about the way that the Irish Church was run, told Henry II that he would like him to invade. But Henry was too busy elsewhere. It was after a dispute between two Irish kings that the Normans began to get involved.

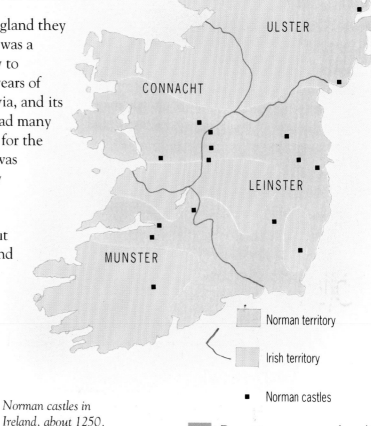

Norman castles in Ireland, about 1250.

In 1152 **Dermot MacMurrough**, the King of Leinster, stole the wife of a rival king, **Tiernan O'Rourke**. MacMurrough returned O'Rourke's wife but O'Rourke wanted revenge and asked the High King, **Rory O'Connor** for help. O'Connor soon defeated MacMurrough and, in 1166, drove him out of Ireland. MacMurrough went to England and asked King Henry II to help him regain his lands.

Henry did not get involved, but agreed that any Norman knights who wished to help MacMurrough could do so. The most important of those who went was Richard of Clare, Earl of Pembroke. (He was known as 'Strongbow'.) He took with him more than 1,000 soldiers and began to overrun much of Ireland. Soon he had helped MacMurrough become High King. In return, MacMurrough allowed him to marry his daughter and gave him land in Ireland. When MacMurrough died in 1171, Strongbow expected to be made King of Leinster.

A Dermot was a man of warlike spirit, with a voice harsh from shouting in the din of battle. He was a man who preferred to be feared rather than loved.

SOURCE

Description of Dermot MacMurrough by Gerald of Wales, who lived at the same time as Dermot.

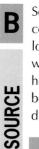

B Some of John's youthful companions sniggered at the long beards of the Irish chiefs who had come to do homage. Then they gave their beards a tug in a most disrespectful way.

SOURCE

Written by Gerald of Wales in 1186.

Henry, however, was becoming concerned about what was happening in Ireland. In England the nobles paid homage to the king for the land they owned. But Strongbow now had land that was outside Henry's control. So he ordered Strongbow to hand over his newly-conquered land. Henry then gave most of it back, in return for knight service – just like in England.

Henry then went to Ireland himself and forced many of the Irish kings to accept him as their lord. Gradually, more Normans began to settle in Ireland. In 1185, Henry sent his youngest son, John, (see pages 26–27) to govern those parts of Ireland that were under the control of the English Church. The English occupation of Ireland had begun.

C **SOURCE**

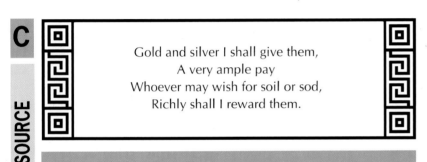

Gold and silver I shall give them,
A very ample pay
Whoever may wish for soil or sod,
Richly shall I reward them.

A poem that Dermot MacMurrough is said to have written to encourage the Normans to help him.

D **SOURCE**

Trim Castle. One of the castles built by Henry II to keep order in Ireland.

Activities...

1 Listed below are some statements about the Norman invasion of Ireland. The name at the beginning of each statement is missing. Also, the statements are not in **chronological** order (the order in which things happened). Copy the statements into your book and put them in the correct order. Don't forget to fill in the missing names!

   a _____ was better known as 'Strongbow'.
   b _____ had his wife stolen by Dermot MacMurrough.
   c _____ drove MacMurrough out of Ireland.
   d _____ talked of invading Ireland but never did.
   e _____ was worried about the Irish Church.
   f _____ asked Henry II for help.
   g _____ made the Irish accept him as their lord.
   h _____ was sent by his father to govern Ireland.

2 MacMurrough wrote a poem, asking the Normans to help him. Write a poem of your own which you think would tempt them to help you. You might like to mount it on a colourful background like Source C.

3 Henry's son John was not popular with the Irish and had to be brought home. Does Source B help you to understand why? Explain your answer.

3.7 Edward I and Wales

When the Normans conquered England, they did not advance into Wales. Instead, William the Conqueror set up the three great **Earldoms** of Chester, Shrewsbury and Hereford along the Welsh Marches (borders). William let these **Marcher Lords**, as they were known, have special powers. They could raise their own taxes, have their own armies and build their own castles. Soon they were strong enough to attack Wales and by the time Edward I became king in 1272, all of south Wales was in their hands.

The mountains of north Wales made it a much harder area to capture. Here, a powerful Prince called **Llewelyn** ruled from his lands in **Gwynedd**. However, Llewelyn was prepared to do homage to the English kings, and in 1267 Henry III gave him the title Prince of Wales.

But when Henry III died, Llewelyn seems to have had a change of heart. He did not attend Edward I's coronation and refused to renew his homage to the new king. So Edward decided to force Llewelyn to obey him. In 1277, he sent three separate armies into north Wales and soon surrounded the Welsh in the mountains of Snowdonia. Edward did not try to fight in this difficult area. Instead, he cut off Llewelyn's food supplies and forced him to surrender.

A SOURCE

David was condemned to be hanged, drawn and quartered. His body was then distributed to four parts of the country and his head sent to join Llewelyn's at the Tower of London. His head had been cut off and fixed on a spike six months earlier.

The end of the Llewelyns. From 'Medieval Britain' by D. Richards and A.D. Ellis, 1973.

B SOURCE

Some 400 skilled masons were continuously at work, and 1,000 unskilled labourers assisted them. There were also 200 carters, 30 smiths and carpenters and a guard of 30 men. Great stone blocks were brought to Caernarvon by sea; 30 boats and 160 wagons were needed to keep the builders supplied.

A report on the building of Caernarfon Castle which was sent to Edward in 1296.

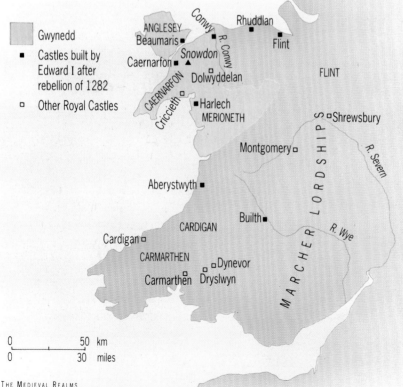

Edward I's castle building in Wales. The counties shown were created by the Statute of Wales in 1284.

- Gwynedd
- ■ Castles built by Edward I after rebellion of 1282
- □ Other Royal Castles

Beaumaris Castle, built in 1295. The latest in castle technology!

Although Edward built some royal castles to keep an eye on Llewelyn, he did not treat Llewelyn harshly and allowed him to stay as Prince of Wales. But in 1282, Llewelyn's brother, David, persuaded him to rebel once again. Again Edward sent troops and defeated the Welsh. Llewelyn was killed in battle and his brother was captured and executed.

To make sure that there were no more rebellions, Edward built a chain of castles around north Wales. They were the strongest castles ever built by the English and could withstand all the siege weapons used at the time. Edward also divided Wales into counties with English laws, courts and sheriffs. But he also tried to please the Welsh. In 1301, he gave his son, the future Edward II, the title 'Prince of Wales' in a ceremony at Caernarfon Castle. Today, the monarch's eldest son is still granted this title.

Yet Welsh resistance did not end totally with Llewelyn. A century later, there was an uprising by **Owen Glendower** who even had support from English forces led by Henry Percy, Earl of Northumberland. However, the rebellion was defeated by Henry IV, though Glendower was never captured. Since then Wales has remained under English rule.

Activities...

Design a newspaper which reports the events in this Unit in the way that a modern newspaper would. Here are some suggestions to help you:

a Decide how many pages you want to include – you might wish to design a colourful first page only.

b Remember to write your account in an interesting and lively way.

c Include lots of sub-headings and colourful pictures.

d Carry out some interviews with people who might have been there at the time.

e If you can, use other books to find out more about:
   • the battles
   • Llewelyn
   • Glendower
     or Edward's castles.

3.8 Robert Bruce and Bannockburn

Edward I was determined that Scotland, too, should be brought under English rule. In 1296, he invaded Scotland and took the Scottish King John prisoner. He said that Scotland was now part of England and there would be no more Scottish kings.

But when Edward returned to England, the Scots rebelled. So Edward marched north again and defeated the rebels. Their leader, William Wallace, was captured and hanged. No wonder Edward became known as **the Hammer of the Scots**.

In spite of this, the Scots were still not prepared to accept English rule. In 1305, some of the nobles secretly crowned **Robert Bruce** as King of Scotland. Bruce seemed to have an impossible task. He had no palace, and all the important castles were in the hands of the English. His army began to disappear as he suffered a series of defeats at the hands of the English. Soon he was forced to leave mainland Scotland and hide on a remote island off the coast of Ireland.

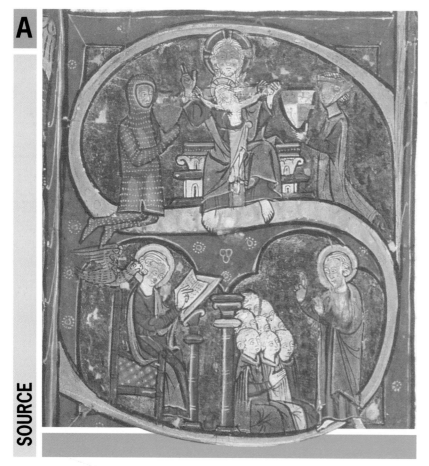

Edward I with his first wife, Eleanor. An illustration from an illuminated manuscript.

The great seal of Robert Bruce, 1326. Here he is shown as a warrior. On the other side he is shown as a crowned king.

The Declaration of Arbroath, 1320.

For as long as one hundred of us remain alive we shall never submit to English rule. For it is not for glory or riches or honour that we fight; it is for freedom alone. The freedom that a true man will give up only with his life.

A section of the Declaration sent to the Pope by a group of leading Scottish nobles. It shows how determined they were to be independent.

In 1307, Bruce's luck took a turn for the better. Shortly after returning to Scotland he heard that Edward I was dead. The new King, Edward II, was much less interested in military glory and he left Scotland as soon as he could. Bruce was now able to recapture the Scottish castles one by one. When he began besieging Scotland's greatest castle at Stirling, Edward had no choice but to march north to save it.

So it was that in June 1314, Bruce's army faced Edward's at **Bannockburn**, just south of Stirling. The result was a great victory for the Scots. It was said that Scotland became rich in one day as the contents of the English supply-wagons were distributed. Although Edward refused to accept defeat, the threat to Scotland ended when he was murdered in 1327. In the next year the new King, Edward III, agreed that Scotland was 'a free and independent nation'. Bruce had won back Scotland's independence.

While he was hiding from the English, Bruce is said to have seen a spider at work. A legend has grown up around this.

One day as Bruce was hiding in a cave he saw a spider trying to make a web. The web kept breaking and the spider kept having to start again. After many attempts the web was made. Bruce knew then that he also had to keep trying and perhaps, one day, he too would be successful.

Activities...

1 **a** Why was Edward I known as 'the Hammer of the Scots'?
  b How was Edward II different from his father?

2 **a** What was so important about the Battle of Bannockburn?
  b With the help of a friend write an imaginary interview with Robert Bruce. Don't forget to include questions about his difficulties when he first became king. Ask him to explain the strange story about the spider!

3 **a** What exactly did the Scottish nobles mean when they wrote the Declaration of Arbroath?
  b Rewrite the Declaration in your own words. Draw a scroll to put the words on.

4.1 Medieval Warfare

When William the Conqueror defeated the English at the Battle of Hastings, he was helped by the skill of his **knights**. The knights were the best soldiers in the army. They wore armour to protect them, and sometimes their horses wore it too. When they charged, they could kill many men with their lances and swords.

Part of a knight's training was to take part in mock battles during **tournaments**. Here they would practice knocking opponents off their horses. These tournaments were great social occasions, with large crowds watching the sport. Since the knights all looked the same in armour, each had his own brightly-coloured badge for identification. A knight wore this on his armour and shield. Later such badges developed into coats-of-arms which some families still have today.

Knights continued to be the most important soldiers throughout the Middle Ages, but most of the soldiers in an army were **infantry** (foot soldiers). They fought in hand-to-hand combat with the enemy using pikes, swords, axes and daggers. However, the English infantry were also very skilled in the use of the longbow. An arrow fired from a longbow could pierce armour even at a distance of 200 metres. French infantry used the more powerful crossbow, but this took much longer to load.

Major battles were not common, and most of the fighting involved besieging (attacking) castles. Special weapons were developed to do this. Sometimes, scaling ladders or seige towers were used to try to go over the top of the walls.

Richard I's coat-of-arms. The lion reflects his nickname of 'Lionheart' – a man who was as brave as a lion. Later this emblem was used by all the Kings of England.

Two knights in a jousting competition, from a 13th-century manuscript.

B

The Battle of Crecy, 1346. A victory for the English longbow over the French crossbow. Notice that because Edward III claimed to be King of England and France, his flag shows the emblems of both countries. From a 15th-century edition of Froissart's Chronicle.

Catapults fired huge rocks to break the walls – or a battering ram tried to knock down the doors. If attackers could not go over the walls or through them, they sometimes employed miners to dig under the walls to make them fall down. But, in the end, attackers often just camped around the castle and starved the defenders out. Then, in the middle of the 15th century, cannon were developed that could blast through castle walls. The age of the castle was over.

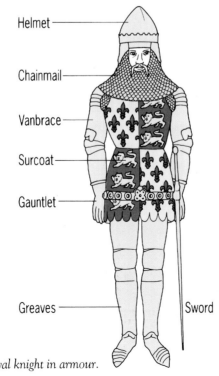

Helmet

Chainmail

Vanbrace

Surcoat

Gauntlet

Greaves — Sword

A medieval knight in armour.

Activities...

1 **a** Copy the diagram of the medieval knight into your books.
   b What do you think it might have been like to wear a suit of armour?

2 **a** Why were knights such difficult opponents in battle?
   b What was the best way of defeating them?

3 Imagine that you are part of an army besieging a castle. Write a diary and explain how you tried to break into the castle. Describe what the defenders would have done to stop you.

4.2 Crime and Punishment

Today, if we break the law, we expect to go to court. If our crimes are serious, we will be tried by a judge and jury. But in medieval times there were very few juries. Henry II thought there should be more, and set up special courts that had judges and juries. Yet even then many people carried on the old Saxon ways of deciding whether a person was guilty or not.

People thought that the best way to test the person accused was by **ordeal**. In ordeal by fire, the accused had to carry a piece of red hot iron and take three steps. Then the burned hand was bandaged. If the wound was not infected after three days, the person was innocent. In ordeal by boiling water, the accused had to take a stone out of boiling water. Ordeal by water meant being tied up and thrown into the river. If the person floated then he or she was guilty of the crime.

The Normans had their own form of trial by ordeal. They said that if a noble was accused by another noble, he could defend himself in ordeal by combat. The two nobles, or their 'champions' would fight until either one gave in or was killed. Whoever won was innocent. If the loser survived, he was put to death.

To us, these seem very strange ways of trying to prove a person's guilt. But they were based on the strong religious belief of the time that God would punish the guilty.

The punishments were very harsh. Murderers and burglars were put to death. Usually men were hung and women were burned to death (though nobles were beheaded). Whipping and cutting off parts of the body (**mutilation**) were common. Punishments were designed to stop people doing the same things again – so a pickpocket or a forger would have a hand cut off. Traders who cheated customers were usually made to stand in the pillory or sit in the stocks. Everyone would laugh at them and throw mud or rotten food.

Some of the crimes of medieval times seem strange to us. Women who nagged their husbands were sometimes punished by being ducked in the river. Other women were made to wear a scold's bridle. This had a piece of metal which pinned the tongue down and stopped them talking!

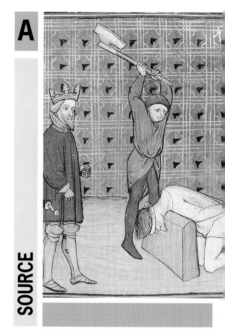

A SOURCE

The king watches somebody being beheaded.

B SOURCE

Execution by hanging.

C

SOURCE

The execution of Earl Waltheof in 1077.
Waltheof asked the executioner to wait until he had said the Lord's
Prayer. He agreed, but when Waltheof came to the last sentence
he sobbed so much that he could not finish the prayer. So the
executioner took out his sword and cut off the Earl's head. Then
the head, after it had been cut off, said 'But deliver us from evil,
Amen.'

From an account by a Norman monk, written in about 1135.

D

SOURCE

*A nun and a monk in the stocks
from an early 14th-century
English manuscript.*

Activities...

1 Four different types of ordeal are mentioned on these pages.
Write down what they are, and describe what would happen in each case.

2 Henry II introduced more juries, but people still carried on using trial by ordeal.
Why do you think this was?

3 Copy out the table below. Now see if you can fill in the punishment you think
would have been given.

Criminal	Crime	Punishment
Will the villein	murder	
John the butcher	selling bad meat	
Lord Robert	killing another noble	
Tom the carpenter	stealing a purse	
Mary the baker's wife	refusing to cook meals	
Robert the villein	stealing fruit from shop	
Jane the miller's wife	murder	

4 'Our system of law today is much better than the medieval system.'
Do you agree or disagree with this statement?

4.3 Religious Beliefs

In medieval times everyone believed in God and the Devil, in heaven and hell. Christians were catholics, and felt that non-catholics were doomed to hell. There were some christians who worshipped God in a different way, such as the **Lollards** (who believed in much more simple worship). Most people felt the Lollards were wrong, and should change their ways. People like the Lollards were often persecuted for their different views.

Most medieval people believed that they might end up being tortured in hell for ever. They thought about this all the time, and it had a big effect on their actions. They tried to show God they were good and tried to avoid the Devil's temptations. How they did this depended on how rich they were, and how they believed it was best to worship God.

Salisbury Cathedral, one of the most magnificent of medieval cathedrals. It was built between 1220 and 1258.

Some people gave money to the poor. Some people were too poor to do anything but try to be kind to others. Many people believed that by serving God as a priest, or a monk, or by going on pilgrimages they would prove that they were good. Many knights fought in the Crusades to fight for God, although there would have been knights who were there just for the fight or to win loot.

People felt the Church had a special relationship with God. Priests carried out services, heard confession and told you what you had to do to be forgiven for the sins you had confessed. Many people gave money to the Church as a way of pleasing God. Cathedrals like Salisbury were built to please God. They were probably also built, like castles, to remind people of the power of the king and nobility.

A medieval painting showing what people thought hell was like. From the 'Bedford Missal' which was made for John, Duke of Bedford in 1430.

Activities...

1 Here is a list of what some people in medieval times did to avoid going to hell:
   - fought in the Crusades
   - went on pilgrimages
   - gave money to do good things
   - built churches.

   a What would be the advantages and disadvantages of each method?

   b Do you think that people did these things just to avoid going to hell? Explain your answer.

2 The drawing below is a key to Source B.

   a Who is shown as 1, 2, and 3.
   b What do you think is happening in the top half of the picture?
   c What is 6?
   d What is happening in 7?
   e Who is shown in 4 and 5?

3 Which Source, A or B, tells us most about people's attitude to religion in the Middle Ages? Give reasons for your answer.

4.4 Life in a Medieval Monastery

Monks and nuns were men and women who lived cut off from the world, serving God. Monks lived in monasteries, nuns lived in nunneries. They lived according to the rules of St Benedict. He said that being a monk was not just about praying and studying, hard work was important too. They were supposed to give up their possessions, eat only the simplest food, wear only the simplest clothes and sleep in a bare cell. They kept nothing from their old lives – names, possessions or social status. Despite this, many people wanted to be monks or nuns. They felt they would be bound to get to heaven if they lived this way on earth. Some wanted to join because, despite the hardships, it gave them a group to belong to. They were provided for, even if it was at a very basic level. Many rich people chose this life, or had it chosen for them when they were young.

Monasteries became rich as they received gifts from people who wanted to give something to the church. As they got richer, they also became less strict. They spent more time managinging their money, and enjoying life, than they did at prayer. The medieval period lasted a long time, and monks and nuns were much stricter just after the Norman Conquest than they were during the Wars of the Roses.

Despite trying to cut themselves off from the world, monasteries and nunneries had a big effect on it. They owned a lot of land, affecting the ordinary people who worked on it.

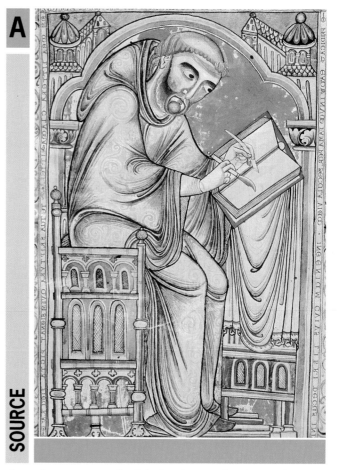

A monk copying out a book by hand. It would take months to copy one book.

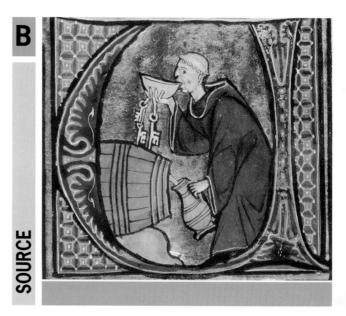

The cellarer. This monk looked after the food and drink in the monastery.

The monks could read and write. They produced most of the books. Books were written, or copied, by hand and decorated with the sorts of illustrations you will find all through this book. Many monasteries had schools, mostly for the children of the nobility. So they could influence powerful people from an early age. Also, many monks were from rich families; they could influence their relations. There were no hospitals at the time. Often it was the monks who cared for the sick. They grew herbs, and kept records of cures that had worked. They also helped the poor and sheltered travellers.

C

SOURCE

All monks shall take turns to wait on each other so that no one is excused kitchen work.

Above all care must be taken of the sick.

Laziness is the enemy of the soul. So the monks should be busy with manual work or holy reading.

A mattress, woollen blanket and pillow is enough for bedding.

Some of the rules of St Benedict.

D

SOURCE

A typical day in the monastery

1.45 a.m.	Get up. Private reading and prayer
2.00 a.m.	Church service
3.30 a.m.	Sleep (summer only)
4.00 a.m.	Church service
5.00 a.m.	Private reading and prayer
6.00 a.m.	Church service
6.45 a.m.	Meal
7.00 a.m.	Work
8.00 a.m.	Church service
9.15 a.m.	Work
11.15 a.m.	Church service
12.00 p.m	Midday Meal
1.00 p.m.	Private reading and prayer
1.45 p.m.	Sleep (summer only)
2.45 p.m.	Church service
3.00 p.m.	Work
5.45 p.m.	Meal
6.00 p.m.	Church service
7.15 p.m.	Private reading and prayer
7.45 p.m.	Church service
8.00 p.m.	Go to bed

Activities...

1 Many of the jobs done by monks are mentioned in this Unit. Make a list of them.

2 What other jobs do you think needed to be done to keep the monastery running?

3 Source D shows the daily timetable of a typical monastery. How long did the monks spend on each of these activities?
  a church services
  b work
  c sleep
  d meals
  e private reading or prayer
  f leisure time?

4 Do any of Sources A–D suggest that monks sometimes broke the rules? Explain your answer.

5 'Monasteries were a very important part of medieval life?' Explain whether you agree or disagree with this statement.

4.5 Life in a Medieval Village

Most villagers in medieval times were **villeins**. These were people who worked the land but did not own it. All the land in the village and surrounding area was owned by the **Lord of the Manor**. He farmed some land himself and let the villeins farm the rest – but there were strict rules about what they had to do in return. To make sure that the villeins did their work the lord appointed a **Reeve**.

Life for the villeins was hard. Fields had to be ploughed and made ready for sowing; corn had to be planted and birds scared away. Once the crops had grown, the whole village joined in the harvest. Then the corn was taken to the mill to be ground into flour.

Winter months were quietest for the villeins. It was then that tasks such as repairing equipment or making furniture were carried out. Sometimes a villein would not have the necessary skill for a job. Then he would get help from one of the village craftspeople, such as the carpenter, blacksmith or thatcher.

Villeins also had to care for their livestock. Sheep and cattle grazed on the village common in the summer, but in the winter there was not enough food to feed them. So many of them were slaughtered and their meat salted to make it last. Sometimes there was not even enough food to feed the villagers.

SITUATION VACANT

Required 1 Villein

Must be prepared to:
1. Pay taxes to the Lord
2. Work on the Lord's land for up to twelve days a year.
3. Never leave the village or let his children be married without the Lord's permission.
4. Agree to grind all his corn in the Lord's mill. (and pay a fee)
5. Not to catch rabbit, deer or any other animals in the wood (they belong to the Lord)

VILLEIN'S CAFE
TODAY'S MENU

Breakfast: Served at dawn. Dry bread & watery ale.
Lunch: served at midday. Bread, a little fish or meat & watery ale.
Supper: served at dusk Thick vegetable soup, bread, fresh fruit watery ale or cider.
SPECIAL if available MILK CHEESE EGGS

A

SOURCE

A Reeve supervising work in the fields.

B

SOURCE

February: ploughing.

In the summer there were plenty of vegetables and fresh fruit, but as winter drew on and the salted autumn meat ran out, times became very hard. Villeins lived in simple cottages with no windows and mud floors. Often they were overrun with fleas, rats or mice. The cottages measured only 3 metres by 5 metres and must have been very crowded because the family shared them with their pigs and chickens. The fire was lit on a stone slab in the middle of the cottage – but there was no chimney. The furniture was very simple: a bed of straw, a table and a few stools. All of their tools and equipment were hung on the walls. Around the cottage was a small garden in which vegetables were grown.

Activities...

1. **a** Make a list of the duties that villeins owed to their lords.
   b Which duty do you think the villeins disliked most?
   c If the villeins disliked what they did, why didn't they just change their jobs?

2. **a** Make a list of what you ate yesterday. How does your list compare with the villein's diet?
   b A slice of bread weighs about 25 grams. Villeins ate about 2 kilograms of bread a day. How many slices is that equivalent to?

3. Draw a calendar of a villein's year. Beside each month describe all the jobs a villein would have to do. (Remember that some jobs would be done in more than one month.)

C

SOURCE

April: sowing.

D

SOURCE

July: harvesting.

E

SOURCE

December: pig-killing. Sources C, D, and E are all from a 14th-century calendar.

4.6 Life in a Medieval Town

In medieval Britain, towns were small. Very few had a population of more than 10,000 people. But during this time towns began to grow. Since the Norman Conquest England had not been invaded and the population was rising. Then trade began to increase. Because the towns were the places where people came to buy and sell, they got bigger.

Towns sometimes applied to the king for a **charter**. This freed the townspeople from having to do services for the lord – but such a favour cost of lot of money. A charter also allowed the townspeople (or **burgesses** as they were known then) to protect themselves by building a strong wall all round the town. The only way in was through special gates, which were kept locked at night. If you were outside at night you had to find your own shelter until the morning.

Inside the walls, the streets were crowded and dirty. There were no building or health regulations and no sewers or running water. Rubbish was just thrown into the streets instead of being collected.

There were many different trades in the town. Each one organized itself into a **guild**. Members of the guild made sure that goods were of a high quality and sold for a fair price. Members also helped each other when one of them was sick or in need.

Any craftspeople who wanted to work in the town had to be in the guild – but there were strict rules about joining. When you first joined a guild, you had to learn your trade as an **apprentice**. After seven years you became a **journeyman** and could earn wages. If you wanted to become a **master craftsman** you had to have your work passed by the guild leaders and pay a large sum of money. Most journeymen could not afford to do this.

> ### Rules of the Hatters' Guild.
>
> 1 No one shall make or sell hats unless he is a member of the guild.
> 2 Only men who enter an apprenticeship under a master may enter the trade.
> 3 An apprentice must serve at least seven years before he may become a journeyman.

A medieval street sign.

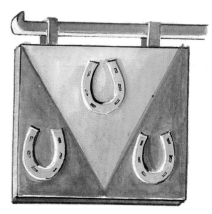

A

SOURCE

Inside a medieval shop. From a 15th-century wall painting.

The town's streets were often named after the groups of craftspeople who worked there. But it was no good putting up a sign saying 'Butcher Sreet' because people could not read! Instead a sign was designed to show what was being sold. As well as having regular shops, most towns held markets. Perhaps once a week outside traders would pay a fee to set up stalls and sell their goods in the town.

But the real highlight of the year was the annual **fair** held in some of the larger towns. Then, merchants from all over Europe displayed their goods. Wealthy people came to see the latest fashions and to buy their silks, jewels and other luxuries. The poor could not afford such things, but they loved the entertainment that came with the fair. Dancing, singing, bear-baiting and wrestling were just a few of the attractions. A great deal of ale (beer) was drunk and often fighting broke out.

Activities...

1 During medieval times many people moved from the countryside to the towns. What would be:
 a the advantages
 b the disadvantages of living in a town?

2 What were the differences between an apprentice, a journeyman and a master craftsman?

3 a Use your dictionary to help you look up what jobs were done by the following craftspeople:
Tanner	Fuller
Carter	Fletcher
Cooper	Mason
Thatcher	Potter
 b Using the street sign as a guide, design a sign for a street where one of these crafts took place.
 c There are lots of people today with names such as Miller or Archer. Where do you think these names come from?

B

SOURCE

A walled medieval town, as shown in the 'Luttrell Psalter', a 14th-century English manuscript.

4.7 Women in Medieval Times

Throughout this book you have read about the people who made history during medieval times. Usually they were kings, or nobles, or perhaps bishops. Sometimes we mention the lives of ordinary peasants. Yet we hardly ever read about what women were doing. Why is this?

Much of the information we have about medieval life comes from monks. They were part of the very small group of people that could read and write. They wrote about the things they thought were important. Religion interested them and so did the struggles between countries, rulers and nobles. This usually meant writing about men.

The rulers of this time were almost always men and the ones that were most respected were the great warriors. When a king died, his eldest son received (or **inherited**) all his father's possessions. Women inherited only when there were no men. This seemed perfectly natural to people at a time when ruling a country often involved leading an army into battle.

The women you do read about are the wives of kings or have become heads of their families because a man has died. They would have been seen by people at the time as 'women doing men's jobs.'

B SOURCE

Queen Matilda

In 1135 Henry I named his daughter Matilda as heir to the throne (his only son William was already dead). But the idea of a woman ruler was not popular and many of the lords preferred Henry's nephew, Stephen. After nineteen years of fighting it was agreed that Stephen should be king, but that Matilda's son, Henry should rule after him.

C SOURCE

Eleanor of Aquitaine

King Henry II ruled over a huge empire which included England and parts of France. When he married Eleanor, Countess of Aquitaine, he added her vast territory to his empire.

A SOURCE

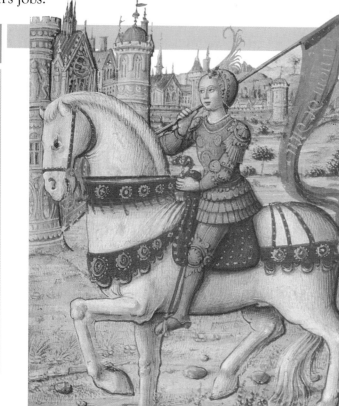

Joan of Arc was a French girl who claimed to hear orders from God telling her to save France from the English. She persuaded the French King to let her ride into battle with his army. The soldiers saw her as a heroine. However she was later taken prisoner and handed over to the English. They burned her as a witch.

For most women life involved getting married, having children and running the home. But there was a great deal more to their lives as well. Some had to earn a living by spinning wool or making cloth; others would work on the land with their husbands. Of course if a woman's husband was away at war, his work had to be done as well. Rich women normally had servants to run their households, but they were expected to defend their homes if their husbands were not there.

F SOURCE

A woman blacksmith, 1330.

D SOURCE

A woman milking a cow.

E SOURCE

A woman making a net, from a 15th-century manuscript.

Activities...

1 **a** Information about medieval life was written down by monks. Why didn't they tell us more about women?
   b 'Women were mentioned if they were doing men's work.' Using Sources A, B and C explain whether you agree with this statement.

2 'Unless they were rich, women only did the housework. Men did all the hard work.' Explain whether you agree or disagree with this statement.

3 Do you think it is still true today that most women who become famous are doing men's work?

4.8 Medicine

Today when we are ill we make an appointment at the doctor's. Usually the doctor gives us some medicine and we get better. But in medieval times there were few doctors and only the rich could afford their fees. Even they were often too frightened to visit a doctor, because sometimes the recommended cure was more likely to result in death than the illness!

Doctors did not really understand how the body worked. They found it hard to learn more because many people did not believe in medicine at all. For example, priests told their parishioners that if they were ill it was because God was punishing their sins. If they wanted to get better then they had to lead better lives.

Many people simply relied on the old methods that their parents and grandparents had used. Some of these methods, like using lucky charms and magic spells, were useless. Others, involving the use of herbs and natural remedies, proved quite effective.

A SOURCE

A woman surgeon performing a caesarian birth. Many women died in childbirth. Very few would have survived a caesarian operation.

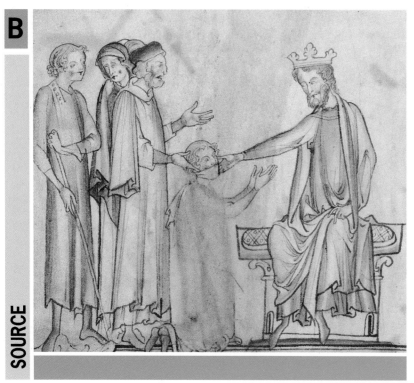

B SOURCE

C SOURCE

I know that your bedside is beseiged by doctors and naturally this fills me with fear. Remember what that unfortunate Roman, Pliny, has written on his tombstone. 'I died of too many physicians'.

Letter to the Pope from the Italian poet, Petrarch, written in about 1350.

◀ *Edward the Confessor cures by touch. Kings were believed to be able to cure illness, particularly the skin disease scrofula, just by touching the ill person. From a 13th-century manuscript.*

The monks who looked after sick travellers in the monasteries were very skilled in using herbs. Some modern medicines are based on the herbs used in medieval times.

Because there was a lot of warfare, doctors became quite skilled at treating wounds. One of the most successful methods was to seal the wound using a red hot poker. This was called **cauterization**. However, because there were no anaesthetics at the time, any more extensive surgery often made the patient die of shock. There were no antiseptics either, so even if people survived an operation they usually died from infections in their wound.

People thought that some illnesses, like fever, were caused because the patient had too much blood. The cure was to remove blood by cutting an artery or using blood-sucking leeches. From the 'Luttrell Psalter', a 14th-century manuscript.

Activities...

1 Give three reasons why people at this time were not keen to use doctors.

2 **a** Why did skills in surgery develop at this time?
   b What were the two major obstacles to successful surgery?

3 Below is a list of illnesses and the cures used for them.
   They need sorting into correct pairs. Some of the answers are in this Unit – others you will have to work out for yourself.

Illness	Cure
Madness	Blood-letting
Warts	Use a hot plaster of pigeon's dung and honey
Coughing	Swallow a heart-shaped herb
Toothache	Putting goat's cheese on your head
Fever	Holding your breath to warm your lungs
Heart disease	Cut a hole in your head to let the badness out
Scrofula	Using a burning candle and water
Kidney stones	Using magic charms
Headache	Being touched by the king

Take a candle of mutton-fat, and burn it as close as possible to the tooth. Hold a basin of cold water beneath it. The worms that are gnawing the tooth will fall into the water to escape the heat of the candle.

A cure for toothache by Rhys Grig, a medieval healer. He died in 1324.

Wart-charmers can be found among country people today. They make warts disappear. Nowadays we find this mysterious, but to medieval people it was quite straightforward, because they believed in good spirits which produced cures.

From a modern history book, written in 1976.

4.9 The Development of the English Language

Sometimes you may not be sure how to spell a word, so you ask your teacher for the 'correct' spelling, or you look it up in a dictionary. You can do this because we all accept that there is a correct version of our language. But at the beginning of the medieval period, people spoke many different forms of English. As each new group of settlers came to this country they brought with them a new language. Over time, these languages got mixed together. This is why, in English, we often have two different words for the same thing. Around the country a variety of different **dialects** (the local form of a language) developed, depending on which people settled where.

The diagram below shows the different languages that have helped form the English we speak today. At the time of the birth of Christ most people spoke a form of Gaelic. The Romans brought Latin with them, and when they left Angles and Saxons arrived with their own language. The Roman missionaries, who came to convert the Anglo-Saxons to Christianity, also spoke Latin. The Vikings spoke Norse and finally, after the Norman Conquest, French was spread throughout the country.

So by the beginning of the 13th century a variety of languages were being spoken in England. The king and his barons spoke French, Churchmen used Latin and the ordinary people spoke 'Middle English'. But there were so many dialects that often people from different areas could not understand each other!

A SOURCE

William Caxton learnt that a man who asked for eggies in a Kent public house puzzled the landlady because local people called them eyren.

From 'The Early Modern Age' by E. Snellgrove, 1972.

B SOURCE

She was so charitable and so piteous
She wolde wepe, if that she saw a mous
Caught in a trap.

Chaucer's description of the Prioress in 'The Canterbury Tales'.

How to make 'Middle English Soup'
Ingredients:
Gaelic
Anglo-Saxon
Latin
Norse
French
Method. Add each ingredient to the pot one at a time and stir very slowly until well mixed up.

Although Latin was the language used by monks and scholars, from the beginning of the 14th century there were many books written in English. The most famous of these is 'The Canterbury Tales' by Geoffrey Chaucer. It was written in the London dialect of Middle English in the late 1380s, and is a collection of stories told by pilgrims on their way to Becket's shrine at Canterbury. Middle English is much more like the English we speak today. Can you work out what Chaucer is saying in Source B?

Yet by far the most important event in the development of the English language came with the invention of printing. In 1476, a rich merchant called William Caxton set up a press in London. In the next fifteen years he printed copies of almost 100 different books, most of which were written in English. Now it was no longer necessary to rely on monks copying out books by hand. Of course only a small fraction of the population could read, but the introduction of printing meant that a standard form of written English soon developed. It was to be many years, however, before there was a standard form of spoken English.

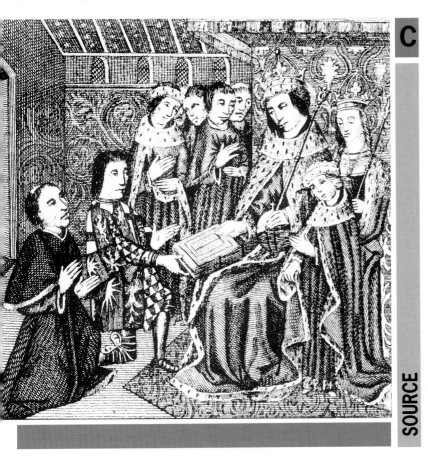

C

SOURCE

William Caxton presents one of his books to Edward IV in 1477. This picture was printed by Caxton himself.

Activities...

1 **a** What is a dialect?
   b Why were there so many different dialects spoken in Medieval England?

2 Today we all speak the same version of the English language, but there are lots of words and phrases which are used in only some parts of the country. Can you think of any which are used only in the area where you live?

3 Below is a list of languages which have helped to form the English language. Copy out the list and beside each language write how it came to England.
   • Gaelic
   • Latin
   • Anglo-Saxon
   • Norse
   • French

4 Explain how the following helped the English language to develop:
   a Geoffrey Chaucer
   b printing.

5.1 The Black Death – the Plague Arrives

In June 1348 a French ship docked in a small Dorset port called Melcombe. It was an ordinary ship carrying ordinary goods to sell in England. But it brought with it something much more deadly. One of the French sailors was ill with the plague. During the next two years more than one third of the people of England would die from this **Black Death**.

The Black Death was really two types of plague. One affected people's lungs and gave then pneumonia. It was spread by germs being passed from one infected person to another. The other type was the most deadly. It was called **bubonic plague** because it caused buboes (swellings) to break out on people's bodies.

Bubonic plague lived in the stomachs of fleas. In turn, these fleas lived in the hair of rats. When the rats died, the fleas often transferred to humans who then caught the disease. Because people at the time did not understand about hygiene, and hardly ever had a bath, they usually had fleas. So the disease spread rapidly.

At first the dead were buried properly in wooden coffins. Soon, so many had died, that new cemeteries had to be made outside city walls where the dead were buried in enormous pits.

A **Causes of the plague - 1**
Saturn, Jupiter and Mars are close to each other. It is always a sign of terrible things to come.

Written by a 14th-century French doctor.

B **Causes of the plague - 2**
God has sent the plague to our town because the people spend so much time gambling, fighting and attending tournaments.

The views of a 14th-century citizen of Leicester.

The spread of the plague

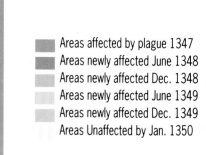

- Areas affected by plague 1347
- Areas newly affected June 1348
- Areas newly affected Dec. 1348
- Areas newly affected June 1349
- Areas newly affected Dec. 1349
- Areas Unaffected by Jan. 1350

People at the time had no idea what caused the Black Death. Indeed, because they had no knowledge of germs, there was no way that they could have understood its cause. So some of the steps that they took to avoid catching the plague, or to cure themselves when they did catch it, seem very strange to us.

C

SOURCE

A priest prays for plague victims. From a 14th-century Franciscan prayer book.

Activities...

1 **a** What were the symptons of bubonic plague?
   b What other type of plague existed?

2 Do Sources A and B help you to understand why people at the time found it so hard to avoid catching the Black Death? Give reasons for your answer.

3 **a** Copy the map into your book.
   b Rewrite this list of towns in the order in which they were struck by the plague:
   Paris Constantinople London Melcombe.
   c What does the map suggest about the way the plague was spread across Europe?

4 Sources A–G show how people tried to cope with the Black Death.
   a Make a list of the methods they used.
   b Which methods do you think were successful?
   c Which methods do you think were unsuccessful?

D

SOURCE

In January 1348 three ships arrived in Genoa. The sailors were horribly infected with plague. When the people of Genoa saw that disease was on board, they drove off the sailors by firing burning arrows.

From a medieval Chronicle.

E

SOURCE

Some tried drinking vinegar, avoiding moist foods or bleeding themselves. Patients were given medicines containing anything from crushed rocks to insects.

Some medical remedies for people suffering from the plague.

F

SOURCE

The terror was such that wives sometimes fled from husbands and mothers from their own children.

Account by a 14th-century Italian poet.

G

SOURCE

You are to make sure that all the human excrement and other filth lying in the streets of the city is removed. You are to make sure that there are no more bad smells for people to die from.

Instructions issued by King Edward III to the Lord Mayor of London, 1349.

5.2 The Black Death – Effects

The Black Death had been a terrifying experience and had brought big changes to England. Throughout the country more than one million people died – perhaps as much as one third of the population. The plague affected everybody, no matter how rich or poor they were. It was worse in the towns, where the overcrowding and filth helped the disease to spread. London's population is thought to have dropped from 70,000 to 40,000 in two years.

In the countryside, some villages simply ceased to exist as all their inhabitants died. Other villages had no one to harvest the crops or to look after the animals. Vast numbers of priests died, and the monasteries were affected even more. Because the monks lived so close together, once the plague got into the monastery, most of them died.

For those who survived, there were some benefits. There was extra land to be claimed now the owners had died. Some villeins managed to become **freemen** because of this. Other villeins simply refused to work for nothing on the lord's land. Labourers began to charge more for their services. The landowners had little choice but to pay the extra wages. There was no one else to hire.

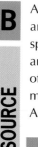

A **SOURCE**

In the north, when the time came for tenants to pay their rents to the Bishop of Durham, no one came from West Thickley. They were all dead .

From 'Medieval Britain' by D. Richards and A. D. Ellis, 1973.

B **SOURCE**

A great plague raged in 1349 and this churchyard was specially consecrated. There are more than 50,000 bodies of the dead here. God have mercy upon their souls. Amen.

An inscription from 1349 found in Spittlecroft churchyard, London.

Percentage of priests who died from the Black Death

50%	49%	49%	48%	44%	39%
Exeter	Winchester	Norwich	Ely	Lincoln	York

In 1351, Parliament was forced to pass a law called the **Statute of Labourers**. This said that wages had to stay at the level they had been before the Black Death, and that labourers could not move from one area to another. Some people just ignored it. People who had survived the Black Death were not frightened by Parliament.

An illustration showing victims of the plague being buried in Tournai in the Netherlands, 1349.

Activities...

1 Explain why the following were so badly hit by the Black Death:
   a priests
   b monks
   c people in towns.

2 The figures for the number of priests and monks who died are probably accurate. The figures for the number of people who died in towns are probably wrong.

   Can you explain why this should be?

3 Source C is a picture showing plague victims being buried in Tournai in the Netherlands. Does this help you to understand the effects of the Black Death?

4 'The Black Death was a total disaster'.
   Do you think that everyone in 1351 would have agreed with this statement? Explain your answer.

5.3 The Peasants' Revolt – Why did it Happen

In 1381 there was a serious rebellion against the king. It was not a rebellion by the nobles, as in earlier reigns. This time it was the peasants who rebelled. Why were they so angry?

One of the peasants' main grumbles concerned the Statute of Labourers. The Black Death had killed so many people that there was a shortage of labourers. Those that survived were able to ask for higher wages. Also, because there was now spare land, some villeins were able to persuade their lords to let them become freemen and receive wages. The new law tried to stop this happening. It even said that people who travelled the country looking for higher wages should be branded with a red-hot iron. So the peasants were very angry.

This was also a time when many peasants began to question what they had been told about their position in life. Their priests had told them that it was God's will that some people were rich and others should have a life of hard work and poverty. Not surprisingly, rich people agreed with the Church. Now men like the priest **John Ball** were saying that this view was wrong, and that the peasants deserved more rewards in life. The Archbishop of Canterbury decided that it was dangerous to let John Ball make such speeches. He had him arrested and put in prison.

But it was King Richard II's attempts to collect extra taxes which eventually sparked off the rebellion. War with France had broken out again in 1369 and Richard desperately needed money to pay for it. So he introduced a **poll tax** which everyone had to pay. His officials toured the country collecting the tax in 1377 and 1380. But the war went badly and English possessions in France were reduced to just a few areas around the coast. When Richard's men started collecting the poll tax again in 1381 there were riots and in some areas the peasants rebelled. This was the start of the **Peasants' Revolt**.

A SOURCE

It seems to me that these evil times are the result of the sins of the people of the earth. Many people think that the Archbishop of Canterbury and the Bishops are to blame. They have allowed some priests to behave shamefully by preaching a false message all over the country and corrupting the people.

The views of Thomas Walsingham, a monk of St Albans abbey writing at the time of the revolt.

B SOURCE

Every man and woman in the realm must work for those who want them and shall only receive the same wages as before the plague.

The Statute of Labourers, 1351.

C SOURCE

We condemn villeins who won't do the services for their lords that they used to. Also they should not come together in great bands to force their lord with violence to agree to their demands.

Act of Parliament, 1377.

King Richard's Poll Tax Demand

All men shall pay the following:

(Married men shall also pay for their wives)

1	In the year 1377	4d
2	In the year 1380	4d
3	In the year 1381	12d

All men resisting are to be thrown in prison.

By order of the King

D **SOURCE**

My friends, the state of England cannot be right until everything is owned by all the people together and there is no difference between nobleman and peasant. We are all descended from our first parents Adam and Eve, so how can they be better than us? Let us go to the king, for he is young, and show him how badly we are treated.

From a speech by John Ball in 1381. Reported in 'Froissart's Chronicle'.

E **SOURCE**

Labourers will no longer be prepared to live on stale vegetables and cheap ale. They demand fresh meat or fish. Unless they are well paid they will complain and curse the king for making a law that harms them.

The views of the peasants.

F **SOURCE**

◄ *John Ball leading a group of peasants. They are carrying the royal standard and the cross of St George to show their loyalty to the king. From 'Froissart's Chronicle'.*

Activities...

1 There had been revolts against the king before. What was different about the Peasants' Revolt?

2 **a** Explain how each of the following helped to bring about the revolt:
   • the Statute of Labourers
   • peasants questioning their position in society
   • the poll tax.
   b Do you think that any one of these reasons was more important than the others? Give reasons for your answer.

3 What do you think John Ball meant when he said we are all descended from Adam and Eve so 'How can they be better than us'?

4 What does Source B tell you about the success of the Statute of Labourers?

5 If you were told that a labourer probably earned only 120d. a year in 1380, would it alter your views about King Richard's poll tax demand? Give reasons for your answer.

5.4 The Peasants' Revolt – What Happened?

During the summer of 1381, there were widespread riots throughout the east of England. In Kent, the rebels attacked Dartford, Rochester and Maidstone, where they chose **Wat Tyler** as their leader. They also broke into the prison and released John Ball. Then they marched towards London and camped at Blackheath, five miles from the city. At the same time a similar peasant army began to march towards London from Essex.

The two armies had very poor weapons and the peasants were not experienced soldiers, but between they made up a force of 60,000 men. They also had the support of the people. When they entered London, people gave them food and drink. What if the two armies joined together? How could they be stopped?

B SOURCE

Richard asked the peasants what they wanted. They replied: 'We want you set us free forever, us and our children and our lands.' Richard said they would be free and would have their will.

From the 'Anonimalle Chronicle', 1381.

C SOURCE

Oh you wretched men, detestable on land and sea. You who seek equality with lords are not worthy to live. Villeins you were and villeins you shall remain.

King Richard's comments to the rebels. Reported by Thomas Walsingham, 1381.

D SOURCE

Tyler stabbed the mayor with his dagger, but the mayor was wearing armour under his robes and was not harmed. He drew his sword and struck back. He gave Tyler a deep cut on the neck and then a great cut on the head. One of the king's followers drew his sword and ran Tyler two or three times through the body, killing him.

The death of Wat Tyler as reported in the 'Anonimalle Chronicle' in 1381.

A SOURCE

◀ A 15th-century painting showing the murder of the Archbishop of Canterbury.

The death of Wat Tyler. On the left Richard sees Tyler killed. On the right Richard rides towards the peasant soldiers who kneel and beg forgiveness, from 'Froissart's Chronicle'.

When King Richard II heard that the rebels were in London he decided to meet them. First he rode to Mile End to meet the Essex rebels. When he promised to grant their wishes, many of the rebels went home. But the Kent rebels were becoming more violent. They broke into the Tower of London and murdered the Archbishop of Canterbury. Then they began to kill tax collectors, lawyers and foreign merchants.

When Richard finally met the Kent rebels at Smithfield he must have been worried about his own safety. But it was Tyler who died that day. Some accounts say that Tyler deliberately insulted the king; others that the king's followers had arranged to kill Tyler anyway. When the rebels saw their leader killed they began to prepare to attack the king's party. But Richard called to them 'Sirs, will you shoot your King? I shall be your captain and you shall have from me what you seek.' He led them out of the city and they agreed to go home.

The revolt was over, but Richard did not keep his promises. He said that he had been forced to make them against his will. The king's armies rounded up the rebel leaders and hanged them. John Ball was hanged and his body cut in four quarters. There were a few more outbreaks of rebellion, but they soon died out. The revolt was over. But it was not a total failure. The poll tax was never repeated, labourers wages began to rise again and within a hundred years the villeins had been set free from their lords' control.

Activities...

1 **a** Which two counties did the peasant armies come from?
   b Why were the king's supporters worried about the two armies joining together?

2 The Kent rebels murdered the Archbishop of Canterbury, tax collectors, lawyers and foreign merchants. Why do you think they chose these people in particular?

3 Do you think that Source E gives a reliable picture of what happened at Smithfield?

4 Richard told the peasants that he would grant their wishes, but he did not. Does that mean he was lying?

5.5 The Wars of the Roses

In 1454 the **Lancaster** and **York** families went to war. Both were descended from Edward III, and both thought that they had a claim to the throne. The Lancastrian's badge was a red rose, and the Yorkist's badge was a white rose, so the battles between them became known as the **Wars of the Roses.**

From 1399, the Lancastrians had ruled England. But in 1461, Henry VI was overthrown by the Yorkist Edward IV. Henry won his crown back in 1470, only to be murdered a year later. Edward ruled again, and the Yorkists now seemed in command. But even then things did not go smoothly. Edward IV died in 1483, and the 12-year-old Edward V became king. Then he and his younger brother Richard mysteriously disappeared. No one knows what happened to them, but it was widely believed that they were murdered by their uncle, who became King Richard III.

There remained only one leading nobleman in the Lancastrian family. He was Henry Tudor, who had been in exile since the reign of Henry VI. In 1485, Henry returned to England and defeated Richard at the **Battle of Bosworth Field**.

Henry had become king by his success in battle and most people thought that he, too, would soon be overthrown. Yet not only did he survive, but he ruled so well that the Tudors have become the most famous monarchs in English history.

In 1486 Henry married Edward IV's daughter, Elizabeth of York. This was a clever move because it united the families of York and Lancaster. The Wars of the Roses were over.

Henry is sometimes said to have been the first of a new type of king. During his reign the government of England began to change. New laws were passed to control the power of the nobles and the use of government officials helped make the king's rule more efficient. He also handled money matters very well and made himself a rich man.

So successful was Henry VII's rule that when he died in 1509 his son, Henry VIII, succeeded without the slightest opposition.

The battles of the Wars of the Roses

Hexham 1464

Towton 1461

Wakefield 1460

Blore Heath 1459

Ludford 1459

Bosworth 1485

Mortimer's Cross 1461

Tewksbury 1471

Northampton 1460

Edgecote 1469

1455 St Albans
1461

Barnet 1471

LONDON

 Lancastrian victory

Yorkist victory

A The 'new monarchy' of Henry VII was in many ways a successful carrying further of work which had begun under the Yorkist king Edward IV and was continued by Richard III.

SOURCE

A modern historian's assessment of Henry VII's rule.

LANCASTER

HENRY IV 1399-1413
HENRY V 1413-1422
HENRY VI 1422-1461

YORK

HENRY VI   EDWARD IV 1461-70

HENRY VI 1470-71   EDWARD 1470 IV

1471-83

HENRY VI murdered 1471   EDWARD IV   Edward V 1483 ?

HENRY TUDOR   RICHARD III 1483-1485

becomes

RICHARD III killed at the Battle of Bosworth Field.

HENRY VII 1485-1509   ELIZABETH of YORK

both Houses united by marriage

Activities...

1 Copy into your book the red rose of Lancaster and the white rose of York. Beneath each badge list the Kings of England who belonged to each family. Don't forget to include their dates.

2 Look carefully at the diagrams in this Unit. Complete the table opposite by putting the battles of the Wars of the Roses in chronological order:

Battle	Date	Who was king	Who won
St Albans	1455	Henry VI	Yorkists

3 Some historians say that Henry VII was a new type of king.
   a What does this mean?
   b Does Source A agree that what Henry VII did was new?

Alexander II, Pope 7
Anglo-Saxon Chronicle 18, 19
Anselm 20, 21
apprentices 46
Arbroath, Declaration of 35
artefact 4

bailey 14, 15
Ball, John 58, 59, 60
Bannockburn, Battle of 35
Bayeux Tapestry 5, 8, 9
Becket, Thomas 22, 23
Bosworth Field, Battle of 62
Bruce, Robert 34, 35
bubonic plague 54

castles 4, 14, 17, 15, 16, 31, 32
cathedral 4
cauterization 51
Caxton, William 52, 53
charter 46
Chaucer, Geoffrey 52, 53
Christendom 20, 21
Church, the 20–21, 22, 41, 58
Cnut 6
Crecy, Battle of 37
crossbows 36, 37
crusades 24, 26, 41

David, brother of Llewelyn 33
dialects 52
doctors 50, 51
Domesday Survey 18

Edgar 6
Edward 'the Confessor' (1042–66) 6,
    50
Edward I (1272–1307) 26, 29, 32,
    33, 34, 35
Edward II (1307–27) 26, 35
Edward III (1327–77) 26, 35, 37, 55,
    62
Edward IV (1461–83) 53, 62
Edward V (1483) 62, 63
Eleanor of Aquitaine 48
Elizabeth of York 62, 63
Evesham, Battle of 28, 29

fairs 47
feudal system 12, 13
freeman 56

Froissart's Chronicle 37, 59, 61
Fulford, Battle of 8

Gerald of Wales 30
Glendower, Owen 33
Grimm, Edward 18
Great Domesday 46
guilds 46
Gwynedd 32

Halley's Comet 8
Hardrada, Harold, King of Norway 6,
    8, 9
Harold Godwinson 6, 7, 8, 9
Harrying of the North 10, 11
Hastings, Battle of 9, 21, 36
Hereward 'the Wake' 11
Henry I (1100–35) 21, 26, 48
Henry II (1154–89) 22, 26, 30, 31,
    49
Henry III (1216–72) 26, 28, 29, 32
Henry IV (1399–1413) 33, 63
Henry V (1413–22) 63
Henry VI (1422–61, 1470–71) 62,
    63
Henry VII (1485–1509) 62, 63
Henry Percy 33
Holy Land 24
homage 12, 13
housecarls 9

infantry 36

Jerusalem 25
Joan of Arc 48
John (1199–1216) 26, 27, 29, 30, 31
journeymen 46

keeps 14, 16

Labourers, Statute of 57, 58
Lanfranc 21
Lewes, Battle of 29
Little Domesday 18
Llewelyn 32, 33
Lollards 40
longbows 36, 37

Macmurrough, Dermot 30, 31
Magna Carta 27
Marcher Lords 32

master craftsman 46
Matilda 48
monasteries 42–43, 56
monks 39, 42–43, 48, 51, 53, 56
Muslims 24
mottes 14, 15
mutilation 38

O'Connor, Rory 30
ordeal 38
O'Rourke, Tiernan 3

Parliament 27, 28, 29, 57, 58
pilgrims 24, 41
poll tax 58, 61
Pope, the 20, 21, 22, 26, 30, 35, 50
primary sources 4

Reeve 44
Richard I 'the Lionheart' (1189–99)
    24, 25, 26, 36
Richard II (1377–99) 58, 60, 61
Richard III (1483–85) 62, 63
Runnymede 27

Saladin 24, 25
secondary sources 4
St Benedict 42, 43
Stamford Bridge, Battle of 9
Stephen (1135–54) 26, 48
Stirling 35
'Strongbow', (Richard of Clare) 30
surgery 51

tenants 12, 13
Tostig 6, 8, 9
tournaments 36
Tower of London 16
Tyler, Watt 60, 61

Walsingham, Thomas 58, 60
Westminster Abbey 10
William 'the Conqueror' (1066–87)
    6, 7, 8, 9, 10, 11, 12, 14, 18, 21, 26,
    32, 36
William of Malmesbury 10
William II (Rufus) (1087–1100) 4,
    20, 21, 26, 30
William Wallace 34
witan 6